You're Not One Of Us

How I Escaped the Cult and Lived to Tell About It

By Joshua Carpenter

Dedication

This book is for my wife, Candy, who inspires me, feeds me (literally!) and is my biggest fan. She has never stopped encouraging me to bring all that I am to the world. If you get to meet her one day, you will see why she is my favorite person in the whole world.

I am writing this book as a result of a turning point in my life. It was 18 years ago, and I can only now speak about it; the path I took to get to it, and what has happened since. Maybe my story will help someone else. If nothing else, I won't be carrying it around anymore. More importantly, my step-children, whom I love with all of my heart, will know what I was about, and can benefit from what I have learned.

This book is not for the faint of heart, nor is it for young children; if it was a movie, it would most likely be rated "R" for adult content, sexual content, and violence. It bluntly exposes the secrets that kept me and my family dysfunctional. This book is about shining the light on my own mistakes, and my family's. It is about how those mistakes led to learning, and it is about illuminating, at the same time, the greatness that comes along with those learning opportunities.

A Word From My Friend Cullen

Cullen Purser, my dear friend and mentor, writes,

> *"Most people are misfits, living with the skewed idea that everyone else is not a misfit. This book is a story of misfits: misfit fanatics, misfit child of fanatics, misfit lesbian daughter of misfit multiple-personality-disorder/wife of misfit grown child trying to understand where the penis goes. All misfits, hiding in the darkness of isolated ideas."*

I am a successful and loved coach today, and I am still a misfit.

A Note From My Sister, Sarah

About 15 years ago I had what I thought might be the last conversation I would ever have with my brother. The brother you're about to read about. I remember so badly wanting to have a close relationship with him. He was my hero. He had always been. I guess I kept that a secret, because I think he didn't know. I always felt safe when he was around. If it wasn't working, he would fix it. If it was stupid he would point that out to me. If it was a waste of time he would talk me out of it. If it was mean, he would step in front of me and take the pain. If it was a really bad choice he would use every strategy he knew to convince me not to do it. And to me it seemed like he was always right. Yet he never played the "nana nana boo boo" card. He was just glad he had convinced me for my own sake. And he was so smart! I remember wishing I could be as smart as him. In school he aced all of his tests with seemingly no effort.

I remember the day he got a letter in the mail from Harvard University after he had taken his ACT test upon graduating high school. He had scored in the top 99% of students in the United States and Harvard University invited him to come and tour the school to see what they had to offer. I remember my parents being proud of him when he got that letter. And then promptly dismissing the letter in a way that seemed to me, 16 years old at the time, to mean, "Yep. You're a smart kid. Of course they'd want you to come to their school. Now, you should probably get back to work," And that's what he did. He never even considered going. I remember believing at the time that it would have been frowned upon if he had.

He had a beautiful spirit. He was kind. Honest. Very intelligent. And deeply patient. My admiration of him was thorough and well informed.

That's why I was so mystified by the consistent emotional beating he took from our mother and by the equally puzzling way our father emotionally disconnected himself from the abuse, fully aware of it and seemingly incapable or unwilling to do anything about it. I remember thinking at a very young age, "I think Dad's just glad she's not mad at him." And I really couldn't blame him. I did the same thing. I chose to be a chameleon... an emotional and mental shape shifter. A climate neutralizer. Every one of us knew how to check Mom's emotional temperature with our first step into a room (or hers).

And each one of us would take our chosen role in the chemistry we had created. I consistently chose, "Stay out of the line of fire as much as possible. Please Mom at all costs. Even if you know in a very sure way inside of you that what she is doing or saying is wrong. Push back if she's crossing the line into violent abuse or paralyzingly painful personal accusations against someone. But do so with great caution. Always align with her at as many levels as possible. And when necessary lie to yourself and her and everyone else to avoid being one of the ones crying at the end of the day."

While I chose how I would survive, I watched my brother get emotionally destroyed for years by our mother, whose personal pain was poured out on him in what seemed to me to be endless forms of misdirected pay-back. And as he will share with you in this book, he wasn't the only one in the family who received vicious, personal attacks from her.

There were others.

But I can guarantee you, I wasn't one of them. I made sure of that.

What I just wrote feels like a confession. A confession I made about 12 years ago when I began to go deeply into my own healing journey. That process is still underway.

And once again, as I dared to confess I was incredibly broken, without my knowledge, on the other side of the world, my big brother stepped out in front of me to check out the lay of the land. Is it safe to tell the truth? What should you do when you look in the mirror and see yourself broken into a thousand pieces, unsure of absolutely everything? If all that "love" that was showered on you for all those years demands that you act a certain way to continue to receive it - what would happen if you dared to stop acting that way? Should you keep on playing the role you know so well because at least you know how to do that? It has kept you reasonably safe so far... maybe the alternative you never dared to choose would be the disaster you always feared it would be? Maybe this healing process was a stupid idea? Seven years after I began asking those questions I found out what my brother had done to pave the way for me. I found this out when he reconnected with me after 10 years of silence and began to tell me about his experiences since I'd last seen him. And he began to take bolder steps toward change and freedom than he ever had before. He permissioned me to do the same. And he shared every step of his process openly with me.

All that big brother stuff he'd always done? He was still doing it. He never assessed the situation just for himself. I always knew that. He was figuratively hacking down underbrush and blazing a trail so anyone who needed to go that same way would have a safe place to travel. So we would have the opportunity to say, "Hey, if he can do it, I can do it!"

If you picked up this book because you thought, "Maybe this guy figured a few things out so I don't have to muck through it on my own," you nailed it. If you think his pain has nothing to do with yours you're mistaken. If you are at the same place in your healing journey by the end of this book as you are right now at the beginning, I would be surprised.

In his accurate and riveting account of our lives from childhood through his shocking launch into the "real world," my brother shares honestly and without shame the stories that gave me nightmares for years after I left home. And in his masterful way he shares, with humour and appreciation, the beautiful things too. My brother has wisely chosen to acknowledge the things that to this point have not been acknowledged as what they were.... Dark things that were happening in our family simultaneously to a public life of happiness and success. I've noticed that things unacknowledged get louder and nastier. I am glad he has chosen to acknowledge them. They have lost their dark power in my heart.

When he told me he was writing this book, I thought, "Oh crap! Now I'm gonna have to be honest too. Or else call him a liar." And that I couldn't do. I wish that I could say his memories are simply recollections of mistakes made by someone doing their best - and he should simply let it go. It was tempting at first. And then I began to be honest about my lifelong and very recent experiences with my parents and I knew I couldn't do that. They did do their best. And they chose not to listen when I repeatedly asked them to own their abusive choices as just that.

The last conversation I had with my mom was less than a year ago, in 2019. She was upset because I had been encouraging one of my younger brothers to pursue dreams she thought were harmful to him. And in that conversation, she said, "I don't know what is wrong with you and Joshua and Josiah. I wish you guys would just grow up."

"Mom, for me, the struggle is with abuse in our childhood that has never been acknowledged," I replied, "I think all three of us are struggling with that."

She got very angry and she said, "You three don't even know what abuse is! You need to stop being a bunch of weenies and grow up!

It was at that point I realized that phone conversations with my mother were not a wise choice for me anymore. So as my brother stepped in to writing this book I knew it was time for me to stand beside him and acknowledge that his childhood wounds, carrying on right up until he was 27 years old, were devastating. And his healing journey has been remarkable. My pain is different but similar. And I have chosen to heal as well.

This man is a pioneer. His ability to assimilate all of our childhood's beauty and struggle and abuse and wholesomeness and isolation and hard work and laughter and devastating pain into who he is now stuns me. He is one of the few people I know who has woven into himself nearly ALL of his life experiences in a very intentional way. He's blocked out or disregarded almost none of it. Having worked with countless deeply wounded individuals myself, in my profession, I don't think he realizes how amazing that is. His example has caused me to coin a phrase in a desire to describe it. I call his experience "sacred pain." That is his choice. And it is beautiful. I hope that the trail he blazes in this book feels safe to you. It is a freedom journey.

As one of my students has now famously said, "Buckle up!"

Chapter 1   I Am Joshua

January, 1974. The President of the United States, Richard Nixon, refused to hand over the Watergate tapes. In response to the world-wide energy crisis, the UK instituted a three-day work week to limit fuel use. In the US, Daylight Savings Time started 4 months earlier than usual in order to save energy. Gasoline was being rationed in the Netherlands. Also in 1974, in the United States, there would be 3.15 million babies born. On January 10th, in Bemidji, Minnesota, I was one of those babies.

Maybe the other babies were ordinary. Maybe other sons and daughters were welcomed, loved, or neglected, as their case may be. Maybe they were raised as well as could be expected and launched into the world to find their own brave new world.

I was not ordinary; I was celebrated and treasured. Every detail of my birth was important and repeated almost reverently as I grew up, the stories told and retold with each passing year, almost to the point of some kind of worship. I did not personally feel worshipped. It seems that for my Dad, my birth was momentous. But he did not talk about me as a person; I felt more like a product that he had created; that he and Mom had made, and God had gifted to the world.

I was born at *1:10* in the morning, on *1/10*/1974. My Dad wanted to name me Joshua, after the Old Testament Biblical general who never lost a battle. My mom hated that idea. She thought that it sounded like an old man's name. Like Moses or Jedidiah or Amos. She wanted to name me Shiloh. I still did not have a name when Dad went home to sleep after my birth. Instead of getting some much-needed rest, the story goes, he went home and read the entire Book of Joshua, in the Bible. At the end of the book, Joshua 24:29, the Bible verse said,

"After these things Joshua the son of Nun, the servant of the Lord, died, being *110* years old."

Dad dialed my mom's room at the hospital and told her, "Joshua is his name!" She was allowed to pick my middle name, and she chose James, after my Grandpa Robert James Pullar, her father. I would grow to love Robert James; I wanted to be just like him.

The story of my naming is an example of how my dad and mom have always worked together. She, protesting and finishing things; he, ever the visionary, putting mystical and even legendary, Biblical emphasis on things that most families may have found common-place. My dad often repeated that "Joshua" in Hebrew was identical to the name for Jesus, or Yeshua. It means, "God Saves," or "Yahweh is Salvation," depending upon the translation.

Everyone has a story.

This is my story.

After I was born, Leah, Sarah, and Melita, came along in quick succession and, by 1979, it seemed like our family was complete; one boy and three girls growing up in the 80's.

We had a beautiful life growing up, for the most part. We worked hard, taking care of ducks and geese and chickens and goats and even a cow. Every night, Dad would gather us all together for Story Time. Either Dad or Mom would read the story out loud; sometimes it was a Bible story, and sometimes it was a riveting mystery, or a heart-warming nature fantasy. We often gave each other back-rubs, or massaged my dad's feet or shoulders. It was a time of connection and relaxation to get us ready for bed. Sometimes Mom would make a snack. Our favorite snack was popcorn - popped in the black kettle on the stove, with fresh butter melted in a saucepan and poured over the hot, fluffy kernels. Or it might be fresh, hot cookies, or cold, home-made applesauce.

Mom was an amazing homemaker; almost everything on the table was made from scratch, including hot, fresh bread. I can still taste that bread right out of the oven, with butter from our cow slathered over it. She would often make cinnamon rolls fresh on the same day as the bread, and we would wait hungrily for those sweet, spicy treats to come out of the oven. Things taste infinitely better when someone adds love!

My sisters and I played outside a lot; we loved playing with the goats, especially when the babies came in the spring, and we even enjoyed getting hay, or hauling feed, or helping with wood. It was great to be included by the adults and I was always treated as a capable part of the team. I loved that feeling.

The only thing on the whole farm that I did not like was a very tall chicken, a rooster, who seemed to me to be almost as tall as I was. He was very aggressive, and I was afraid of him. He whipped me with his wings if I got too close, or pecked at me. My mom chided me to not be afraid of him, that he could sense my fear, but that didn't help me much.

The only time that I can remember my dad getting angry with me was because of that chicken. Dad sent me to the barn long after it got dark, in the middle of a howling blizzard, to check on the goats. A nanny goat was "kidding" early, and the weather in International Falls, Minnesota was Arctic. Dad had to work the afternoon shift at Boise Cascade, the paper mill in town. He was counting on me to make sure that the baby goats that were coming did not freeze to death in the barn. Mom had recently delivered my little sister, Melita, so she was not able to move much. Melita's delivery had been very traumatic, and the doctor tied Mom's tubes because he said that her body would not survive another pregnancy.

On that nastiest of Minnesota nights, I dutifully bundled my five-year-old body up to the gills and trudged through the deepening drifts out to the barn. I was so afraid that that chicken would be there, and so he was. He was right in the doorway of the barn, staying out of the stinging, wind-driven snow. We locked eyes.

"He can tell you're afraid of him!" I could hear Mom's voice in my head. I couldn't stop being afraid.

The harder I tried to ignore it, the more I felt my fear ramp up. I could see the goat-stall over the tall rooster's shoulder; I could see one corner of the pen, and could see the nanny who was expecting, lying peacefully on the straw in the back corner. She looked fine from where I was. As the rooster began puffing himself out in preparation for kicking my ass (I had experience with this) I made a command decision. I turned and ran like mad through the drifting snow to the house.

When Dad called from the mill, I told him that yes, I had checked; and no, the babies were not born yet.

It was a half-truth that I told to save myself from having to face that chicken, and it almost cost a baby goat his life. When Dad got home after midnight, he went out to the barn in the blizzard and knew immediately that I had lied. There was a baby goat, birthed hours ago in the back corner of the pen. He was frozen solid. When Dad carried it into the house, he was as stiff as a board.

Dad was so angry. He kicked me right in the butt.

The baby goat went right into the oven that night, and I watched with a massive load of guilt as my dad did everything he could to gently bring the kid's body temperature up to normal. Unbelievably, after some time warming up, the tiny goat raised its head and cried for its mamma. Dad already had the nanny goat in our trailer house's linoleum entryway. That kid suckled, lived, and even thrived, despite being frozen solid. I was so relieved, and I resolved to be more brave after that.

Dad never forgot that he had kicked me like that.

Decades later, he shared with me that he always regretted that boot to my backside. He remembered his dad doing that to him, and he was very sorry that he had repeated the harsh punishment with me. I forgave him easily because by the time that he mentioned it again (I was in my twenties) I didn't even remember that he had done it. He seemed relieved. He was generally an extremely patient man; there are no other stories about my dad losing his temper with anyone.

My mom was a bird of a different feather. She was so much fun; and along with her passion for fun and drama, she also had a temper. I remember sitting on the couch with my sisters for hours as she waited for one of us to confess to using the wrong tooth-paste cup. In the end, my middle sister, Sarah, confessed and took the spanking, even though she didn't do it. She just wanted the ordeal to be over. Through pure happenstance, it later came out that Dad was the culprit, and that he had no idea that we kids (and especially Sarah) had suffered for it.

But Mom's temper and harsh punishment style really didn't bother us in those early years, because we wouldn't trade her sparkling personality for anything. Mom tickled, and joked, and teased, and always had an idea for a great party. Throughout much of our lives, any friends that we made wanted to come to our house because Mom was the coolest mom ever.

When I was in my teens, she let us clear the living room of all furniture, and play soccer from wall to wall. It was deep winter outside, and we desperately needed to be active. What a blast.

When I was 11, we were hosting a "Tacky Party" for one of Mom's friends, and she scooped into the popcorn bucket and began throwing popcorn all over the room. If we caught it in our mouths, we ate it. If we didn't catch it, it was the five second rule, and we ate it. We found popcorn under furniture for months.

Mom was all about the party, and if we were faced with an unpleasant task or situation, she would do anything to try to make it fun. Just like Mary Poppins, our favorite family movie, she brought the "spoonful of sugar" that made the medicine go down.

Mom loved to sing. Driving us around the Northland, or Up North, as we called International Falls, Minnesota, and its environs, she often would sing and encourage us to sing along. Once, driving and singing, *"If You're Happy and You Know It Clap Your Hands,"* she was, of course, clapping along. She lost control of the wheel, and the car went into the ditch in front of the neighbor's house. She drove it right back up and out of the ditch; without missing a beat of the song she added, *"And Don't Tell Dad About This.... Clap Your Hands*!!" None of us breathed a word when Dad noticed the deep, muddy ruts in the neighbors' ditch that we had left while we were clapping our hands.

I did not always feel like singing, nor was I as cheerful and energetic as she was, so sometimes I was annoyed that she was so insistent that I sing along. She would badger me until I faked cheerfulness and sang along. Or, after I learned how to whistle, I would whistle along to the tune. The whistling annoyed her, but she sometimes let me do it my way.

We grew up tough and rugged, living out in the woods some twenty miles from International Falls, on a gravel road outside of Littlefork, a tiny farm and lumber town that had a small lumberyard, an elementary school, a grocery store, a few churches and bars, a hardware store, and a little greasy spoon that was literally called the Big Spoon. Besides raising horses, chickens, goats, and many other animals, we cut and carried our own firewood and raised a huge garden every year. We brought in at least ten cords of wood per winter.

We wore out the knees of our jeans playing on the concrete floor of the house that we built mostly ourselves. We picked blueberries in the summer by the gallons (each sibling had to pick a certain amount based upon age; a cup for the 5 year old sister, and a pint for the 7 year old, and so on up the chain). We netted Carp out of the river when they were running heavy, and we ate the dirty fish in patties and other dishes that hid the flavor. We rarely had hamburger, because it was very expensive, but we did eat a lot of vegetables from the huge gardens that we all worked hard in during the short summer.

Nearby International Falls was called the Icebox of the Nation, and was the home of cold-weather testing of all kinds. It was not unusual for the temperature to reach 40 degrees below zero several times each winter, and very commonly it was 20 degrees below zero (Fahrenheit) for longer stretches. Anything below -10 degrees is brutal. In the first home that Mom and Dad lived in (it had been Great Grandma Ella's house originally) the drool would freeze on your pillow while you slept, and the windows had a layer of frost on the inside that became thick ice as our breath froze on them. Rainy Lake froze several feet thick, and cars and trucks drove out on the lake all winter.

During the long winters, we would spend hours every week "getting wood;" trudging through the snow-covered forest and packing freshly-cut firewood into the pick-up or trailer to be hauled home, split, and fed into the wood-stove to keep the house warm. Dad woke up in the night to "feed the stove." If the fire happened to go out overnight, in the morning we would huddle around the stove in our pajamas and blankets, so that the minute that Dad got a roaring fire going, we were ready to warm our hands and backsides.

Getting wood was hard work and often very cold. We bundled up in snowmobile suits ("snowsuits") and heavy winter boots (frozen toes hurt like the dickens when they thawed) and big leather "choppers" with woolen mittens inside for extra warmth. We learned to work and keep moving constantly, creating body heat to ward off the cold and frostbite.

Before my mother "toughened me up," I hated the outdoors. I had thin fingers, I was sensitive to everything and had a body that was a beacon for mosquitoes. I complained about many things in our hard-knock life. My mother expected me to not be such a cry-baby. I was 8 or 9 when an unusually early winter caught us with carrots still in the ground. Before they could freeze solid, we spent a bitterly cold afternoon pulling them up and washing the mud off of each one in a nearby ditch. My fingers quickly burned from the cold water, and my face was whipped and stung by the sharp, bitter wind. My second-hand jacket felt useless. I wanted to stop. I cried. I begged to go inside.

"You BIG BABY!" Mom shouted over the wind. We had to finish. "He who does not work, does not eat!"

I learned not to cry; and to be tough. I cut my leg badly on a bike the summer after I turned 9, and we made a very rare trip to the doctor for me to be stitched up. I was fascinated by the way the fat was hanging out of the hole that I had made in my shin. It required 7 large stitches, and the doctor kept asking me if I was feeling anything, because I was smiling at him while he worked. I had developed the ability to ignore pain almost completely, and I knew that I was expected to be polite to the doctor, so I was smiling at him. This immunity to most types of pain would not serve me well later in life, when I would avoid the doctor at all costs, often resulting in minor conditions turning into bad infections or dangerous blood loss. My siblings are the same way to this day, I believe; it was our culture.

Our strong little family unit would eventually go on to learn a great deal about each other, and from each other. I love each one of those people dearly, and I wouldn't leave the strong family unit that we created until I was 27 years old. We would become pioneers in home-schooling in 1980, start a family Gospel band in 1988, adopt three more children starting in 1989, and travel the country as a singing and preaching family until 2001. It was a fabulous upbringing, and I loved most of it. In the midst of all of the successes and with all of the people who looked up to our family, it took years for me to realize that we had not been, in fact, better than other families.

In our zeal to be excellent, we had covered our dysfunction up cleverly, and later in life that cover-up kept me stuck in the same old patterns.

The glory and power of The Carpenter Family Singers has been well documented, so this book is not about that; it's about the failure. It's about a family of misfits.

Chapter 2   The Pullars

     I was six years old on Tuesday, November 4th, 1980, and Ronald Reagan, who was a distant cousin of my Dad's adoptive Mom, Eula Carpenter, was elected President of The United States of America. Both of my parents' families, the Carpenters and the Pullars, lived within twenty miles of us in and around International Falls.

     I was in first grade, in Mrs. Bloomquist's class, and as Ronald Reagan's campaign built to a head, Mrs. Bloomquist's pupils got to fill out mock ballots of our own, in order to learn about our democratic system. I remember it clearly, because I was only in her class for a short time; after coming home with the "F word," my parents decided to home-school me.

     Staring at the mock ballot and having no idea how to decide, I had voted for Ronald Reagan, because he looked kind. I was very embarrassed that next weekend when I talked about our mock vote and my Uncle Ron Pullar (who was only 11 years older than I) told me that I had voted for the wrong guy.

     I knew nothing of Democrats and Republicans, but Uncle Ron, who I adored (and still do, frankly) tried to explain why it mattered so much. I couldn't follow; something about farmers and wages and foreign policy. I felt bad that I had done it wrong, and that I had chosen the wrong side in what was obviously a very adult debate. I understood that I had not done what my "cool" family members would have done.

My uncles on my mom's side (the Pullars) were so funny. I loved to listen to them telling jokes, gathered around the kitchen island at my Grandma Dori's house. I loved the way my Grandpa Bob would say "Oh, Geez!" and walk away laughing, and shaking his head at whatever punchline one of the boys had just delivered. My mom, Jan, was the second oldest in a family of eight - three girls and five boys, and I loved every one of them. They were just so young and fun.

One holiday, Uncle Dean once came home to the Pullar house unexpectedly from Denver, Colorado. He was the first to move that far away, and was often missed at family gatherings. One of the other boys picked him up at the airport for this particular holiday, and in the chaos that always happened at the front door, Dean quietly slipped down the basement stairs instead of heading upstairs to see Grandma in the kitchen. He had arranged for Steve or Ronny to pick up the phone upstairs while he rang it from the downstairs phone. After one of the boys handed the phone to Grandma, Dean had a long conversation with her about how much he wished he could be there for the holiday, and Grandma went on and on about how she missed him.

"Just a minute," he cut her off. "I think someone's at the door." He set the phone on the workbench downstairs, and quietly climbed the stairs to the kitchen. Grandma was pacing around on the end of the extra-long phone cord that hung off the wall phone above the desk between the dining room and living room.

When Dean popped around the corner she could not, for a few seconds, mentally process that he was not in Denver, and that he was, in fact, standing right in front of her with his signature toothpick and an ear-to-ear grin.

Grandma shrieked, "DEAN!" and threw the phone across the room as we all laughed and celebrated and he swept her into a warm hug.

For a different holiday, Uncle Steve, who was an electrical apprentice in Minneapolis, came home and was greeted by the warm circle of hugs that everyone got when they arrived.

Everyone talked at once, and the chaos led to even higher levels of excitement. As more children and their families arrived, Grandma was quickly becoming overstimulated by the growing number of loved ones in her kitchen.

"Steve, did you have a good trip up?" she asked. He knew that she was wandering already in her mind to the next guest that was arriving, so he said in a downcast tone, "Well, yeah, but I hit a pink elephant with my car."

She was clearly not listening.

"Oh, Steve!" she said, responding to his tone rather than his words, as she headed towards the door to greet Danny and his girlfriend arriving from Hibbing, about 2 hours from the Falls.

"I'm sure glad that you are ok! Is your car ok?"

"Yeah," he deadpanned to the great hilarity of those who were actually listening to him, "But it got pink stuff all over it."

"Oh, no!" as she turned back to the door, "HELLO, Dan and Irene!" and started hugs all around. She turned back to Steve and asked "Can you fix it, you think?"

By now, we were all roaring with laughter while Steve's eyes twinkled with delight. Grandma will likely deny this story to this day, but we love her for it; she just wants to love us all in the best way possible, and sometimes it overwhelms the brain's ability to keep up.

But there is nothing stupid about any of the Pullars: a highly respected pastor; a business woman; a marathon runner; an accomplished shop teacher and track coach; a commercial painter; an electrician who managed the Minneapolis Airport construction project; a male model/commercial actor; an executive assistant; and a hospitality manager for a major hotel chain. These titles barely touch the major contributions the Pullar children have made to society.

I tried so hard to emulate them. I learned to tell jokes like my uncles did at an early age. My first very memorable attempt at age 6 failed, though. I heard one of the uncles tell the story, and in a rush to try my hand, I found another uncle that I figured must not have heard it yet. He listened politely while I carefully repeated the story about the Indians who were having a tea-drinking contest, and how one brave was really good, and beat them all at drinking tea. I wrapped it up with the climax, "The only sad thing was, the next day, they found him dead in his TENT!" And I chortled away uncontrollably.

It took me a bit to realize that he was not laughing with me. He (and everyone else within earshot) was laughing AT me. "Don't you mean they found him dead in his TEA-PEE?" he asked between chuckles. "That's what I said, in his tent!" I was red in the face, and it took me some time (years) to figure out where I had gone wrong. "Listen," he said kindly, "don't you know, you never laugh at your own joke?" I had never thought about that, but I resolved to keep working on my delivery, with all of that in mind. I was not going to be deterred from being every bit as awesome as they were.

Some of my favorite memories as a child are at that house on Highway 53, just outside of International Falls, Minnesota; the house where Grandpa Bob and Grandma Dori and all 8 of the Pullar kids lived, loved, fought, and where Grandma lives to this day. It was where I met one of my best buddies of 40 years, when I was 5 and he was 13.

Shayne Stillar, who grew up across Highway 53 from Grandma and Grandpa, was never supposed to make it. Shayne was born with Aperts Syndrome, and his parents were told that he would not walk, talk, go to school, or maybe even live very long. But Shayne's parents refused to accept that reality.

Today Shayne is a gold medalist in the Senior Olympic games more than once, earning too many Cycling and other trophies for me to count here. He finished college, and held down jobs. And more than that, he is a kind and generous human being who has used his triumph over the odds to encourage others who are struggling with a "disability."

Shayne is a great example of the kind of people that I grew up with. Extremely tough people. Grandpa Bob is the toughest man I have ever met, and while I see myself as pretty hardy, I could not match his ability to work in the bitter cold, or stifling humidity, or withstand mosquito torture, or put in long hours, not stopping until the work was done. Whatever it took.

Growing up in this environment, you could get dunked in a rain barrel (me), challenged to drink water until you threw up (my Uncle Dean, who was then told that no one else would drink, because he won!), stuffed in a barrel and rolled down a big hill (my Uncle Danny), a face "washing" in a snowbank (me again, and I'm sure EVERYONE ELSE), snapped with dish towels that had been carefully wetted so they would draw blood (again, me, and probably everyone), or any number of physical tortures.

The Pullar kids were wild and tough, and I am sure there is much more that has not been told. If the stories are to be believed, the neighbor lady used to push her kids outside in the morning and then lock the door for the day to clean the house and have her own time. Those who lived through it, got tough.

That white house with the green trim on Highway 53 was a free for all. And the rough horseplay was nothing compared to the way that the kids destroyed each other with words. This was where I learned to beat someone emotionally.

The Pullars were like the Brady Bunch without the warm, fuzzy filter. It was "teasing," and it was a sure sign that they liked you if they teased you. The boys called my mom "Buffalo Butt" because she hated it. Uncle Danny wore two pairs of jeans, because he could not endure the teasing if his zipper happened to come down. He was teased even harder for the extra pair of jeans. My uncles were famous for complimenting girls with, "For a fat girl, you don't sweat much!" or, "Stick with me, Baby, and you'll be farting through silk!"

Many who joined the family as spouses or love interests were quite taken aback by the harsh environment. Uncle Danny, home with his college girlfriend, asked one of the other boys to "Come at me!" with the three-wheeler. As the speeding ATV reached Dan, he leaped and attempted to clear the other brother. He almost made it, but his feet caught, and he did a spectacular cartwheel in mid-air, while his new girlfriend screamed, "Sue him, Dan! Sue him!" Dan came to, brushed himself off and laughed. That girlfriend didn't last.

I was a very soft-hearted boy, but by the time that I was in my teens, I knew how to argue, defend, debate, and verbally eviscerate any opponent that I might come across. It was survival. I needed to know my adversary; what were they self-conscious about? Where had they failed? What string could I pull out of their psyche that would leave them speechless, or hurt, or too angry to respond?

Maybe my opponent was overweight. That was an easy one, and it wasn't until I watched one of my sisters battle her weight and used it against her that I saw how truly devastating that weapon was. I never did that again after seeing the pain in her eyes; but the damage was done.

Maybe my foe had a big nose, odd clothing, or struggled with grades in school. Anything that bothered them or stuck out as unusual I could use to turn an argument in my favor. It needed to be personal; I needed to get under their skin. It was a constant battle for dominance.

At the time, it was fun; competitive, and very entertaining. My Grandparents were incredibly tough, and they raised a house full of tough kids. I admire them deeply for that.

When my parents and siblings and I formed The Carpenter Family Singers, the Pullars would become some of our best fans. My mom had been a wishful singer when she was in her teens, and she supported us kids heavily in this endeavor. We started at a Mother's Day Banquet at a friend's church, and it grew from there. One performance led to the next, and we became a nationally-touring Gospel group. We preached family values, and we sang about Jesus. We loved our music, our fans, and each other. But this habit of verbally destroying each other was not going to end well.

Jump ahead with me to 1999.

If you, like my Grandpa and Grandma Pullar, were watching Good Morning America with your eggs and coffee, you know that in the US, President Bill Clinton was impeached and subsequently acquitted of perjury and obstruction of justice charges. Spongebob Squarepants premiered on May 1, and the Dow Jones Industrial Average would break 11,000 for the first time in history. Lance Armstrong won the Tour De France, Boris Yeltsin resigned as the president of Russia, giving way to Vladimir Putin, and the Columbine High School Massacre left a dark stain on the American memory. A gun control bill failed to pass in the U.S. later that year.

I was 25 years old and The Carpenter Family Singers were performing at the Hart Ranch Arena. We had no time or attention for the news. We were doing a regular show there, 3 nights every week, with ticket sales funding our family's music career. Each of us adult children had full time jobs as well as the demanding concert schedule, and all of our money went into the Band. By then, we had adopted three children, who joined the show. In general, we all loved traveling and working together.

On tour, I played the piano, stage right, in my tuxedo. Standing immediately to my right, my 6' tall, curvy, blonde, charismatic sister, Leah, played the guitar and charmed everyone. Leah is 18 months younger than I, and we were best friends most of our young adult lives; she has a natural, brilliant energy and was absolutely critical to the way the Band connected with our audiences.

In the center of the stage is my vocally exceptional sister, Sarah. She used to practice with recordings of Mariah Carey. She had a ridiculously incredible range and talent, and would be considered our lead singer. She also ran the sound board and played harmonica.

On the other side of her, stage left, was the youngest of the "Big Kids," Melita. She could play anything. She started all of our preset drum beats - an extremely demanding job. She also played back-up keys, piano, bass guitar, violin, and hammered dulcimer. And anything else she felt like playing. She was technically brilliant. She also managed the back row.

The back row consisted of the youngest three siblings, who were much younger than the other four of us. The "Little Kids" as we called them, came to us because my mom said that she was not ready to plant flowers; she had enjoyed rearing us, and she was intent to do more parenting. Mom did a large amount of paperwork and survived a big learning curve for those first two adoptions, which brought us Josiah and Susanna - six months apart. They were both from Belize, although from very different cultures, races, and family situations.

Jeremiah, from Canada, came to us through a "Mother Initiated Adoption," meaning that Jeremiah's birth mother, Anne, chose the exact family that she wanted her baby to be adopted by. Anne loved our singing and wanted her son to be an American citizen, so she came and lived with us for 6 weeks before his birth, and we all loved her by the time she delivered Jeremiah at our local hospital in Sleepy Eye, Minnesota.

Mom handled every aspect of the adoptions, and was absolutely invested in the process; she was like a pitbull and would not take "no" for an answer. Brown County Social Services made an exception for Jeremiah's adoption, because they did not normally allow three children from separate families to be adopted into one home so close together in time. Mom can be quite persuasive, and she loved the challenge. She was committed to having each of these kids in her home.

That was before "The Carpenter Family Singers" became such a huge part of our lives and so motivating and engaging for my mother as a businessperson. So the "Little Kids" were grafted seamlessly into the show.

The "Little Kids" started their careers being carried on stage as babies, and graduated to a row of stools at the back of the stage. They were adorable, and I still love every one of them. Josiah is a great dancer, and has more charisma in one little finger than I have in my whole body. His foster parents called him Sunny Boy; that was before we took him home at 3 months old. He was a ray of sunshine. He danced, sang, and eventually graduated to playing his guitar on my left (stage right) when he was about 7. He idolized me, and I was honored.

Six months younger than Josiah was Susanna, who is pure Mayan Indian, and extremely powerful. Nothing rattles her, and she eventually moved from the stools to the extreme stage left with Melita, or Skeet, as we nicknamed her. Susanna always had a gorgeous tiny version of the matching "classy" dresses that my sisters were known for wearing (picture any "sister" "country" group from the seventies) and she played keyboard and a tiny accordion.

Jeremiah, the baby of the family, was blonde, blue-eyed, very quiet, and disliked attention; he was, surprisingly, an even better dancer than Josiah. He chose to be a drummer, and with his double joints, he could do things that I could only teach - and then sit back and watch him execute with ease. He was playing the full drum-line to the Christian version of "Louie, Louie" at age 6. He was brilliant, and was always making a gizmo or working gadget out of a toilet paper roll, a rubber band and a paper clip - or whatever else he had at hand. His favorite thing to say was, "Watch this!"

Mom moved in and out of center stage doing most of the speaking. She was like the quarterback for our team - often "calling audibles" and changing the set list as she saw fit. We all liked the way she did it; she had a natural feel for crowds, and would choose music and bits of story that would speak to whomever we were in front of. And she did it on the fly, responding to what she sensed from the crowd in the room; it was a real gift.

Mom also sang, although if I was honest, she wasn't very good, and didn't want to practice or learn what she was lacking. We kids tried to gently suggest some pointers, but anything we said felt like criticism to her and resulted in a blow up, so we learned to leave it alone. And Dad would never have been one to poke the bear. There was no one else in our circle to give her that feedback.

As the show began at the Hart Ranch Arena in 1999, it was a good thing that the opening theater music was pretty loud, because I wasn't entirely sure that the crowd that was entering the arena was not overhearing the shouting and hurled curse words from behind the stage.

My dad, always too passive to really get involved, interrupted; "It's five minutes guys!"

This served only to intensify the parting shots and thrown music sheets, as each one headed to their dressing room to finish wardrobe.

In the ongoing battle backstage, dirty looks and four-letter-words had become personal attacks, and character assassinations. Carpenters were choosing sides, and muttering their case to the buddy that they had chosen on this go-round. Past failures were being dredged up, and tears were starting for someone.

This story has no details, because they would not be accurate, nor would they matter. It was an endless merry-go-round of drama, all predicated upon past hurts and future targets.

What had begun as children "teasing" with our aunts and uncles and Mom, (Dad would never participate) had morphed into our verbally and emotionally destructive normal. Our every desire and ambition had become tied to our ability to destroy our opponent; our focus was bent on getting the others over to our side.

"1 minute, guys!"

Dad sounded impatient and irritated at this constant gouging-of-eyes that went on emotionally; but he did nothing to stop it, as usual. We seldom fought physically; we didn't have to. We were absolute masters of the emotional massacre.

As a tiny example of our verbal viciousness and the long-reaching damage that we did to each other, I offer a story about a time that my little brother, Josiah, who came to us from Belize, was trying to enter into the verbal fray.

This one happened on the tour bus, crowded and hot, with eleven people getting ready for a show, and it involved Cindy, a friend who will factor into my story in a bigger way later. Josiah was only 7, but he was already learning to cut people in two with his words.

Mom was fully involved in these events, often starting them, and she was adept at it. Josiah knew that Mom was angry with Cindy; and he was trying hard to stay on the winning side, (Mom's) and practice the craft. On this day, he looked at Cindy arrogantly and said, "Well I know that you are wrong, because you aren't even a Carpenter anyway!" It was incredibly hurtful, with no obvious logical value. We all stared for a moment; it was not cool to see our worst selves mirrored in this child.

Momentarily, Josiah smirked, taking the sudden full attention of all of the adults to mean that it had been well played. But he had not anticipated the way these things could turn on you. Mom looked at him and spat, "Josiah! That was mean! YOU are not a Carpenter either!"

To a brown-skinned, adopted child who already felt like maybe he did not belong, this mean-spirited comment from the only mom he had ever known was so incredibly destructive in his life.

Josiah, watching a cartoon version of "The Ugly Duckling" at about that same time in his life, had fallen apart, sobbing. The song, *"You're Not One of Us"* tore him up.

"You're not one of us,"

"It's plain to see,"

"When it comes to ducks, you're just uu-uugly.."

Josiah was not the only one who felt *uu-uugly* ...nor was he the only one who would end up feeling like an outsider.

Back in the Hart Ranch Arena, the crowd was on their feet, thundering applause for our entrance. We were trotting on stage, smiling, waving, and launching into our up-beat, positive, opener - all about Saturday Night at the Twist and Shout. We would do what we did almost every night somewhere in the US; singing about family values and preaching about the love of Jesus.

The glares and hurt feelings were still there. But the show must go on. People must continue to think that we were a close and loving Christian family.

We looked smashing! Full tuxes for the guys, even my littlest brother. We each had a matching bowtie, and fancy cummerbunds. And if the guys were fancy, the girls were even more fantastic. Full, lacy dresses with A-line skirts and puffy sleeves, or shaped bodices and chiffon accents. Mom hand-made most of the girls' outfits, and some people thought that we were Mennonite or Mormon because of the dresses. Mom said that we should always dress a little better than our crowd - though many times we were dressed much better than our crowd.

To each other, we could admit that we weren't perfect, as a family. But we were unwilling to seek help from outside our family's isolated Eden. That would require humility, and an openness to getting support. It would mean being open to changing what wasn't working. And we wanted nothing to do with any outside support. We were good. We did not need help. We were committed to our dysfunction; and we were selling the idea that we were practically the perfect family.

Many of our most loyal fans held us up on a pedestal, and felt a deep sense of dysfunction and shame themselves, because their family was doing exactly what we were doing behind closed doors. Destroying each other intentionally. Defending territory. Choosing to strike out rather than get help.

We were misfits; we just hid it better than some did.

Chapter 3
The Carpenter Family

I never heard my Dad's opinion of that election in 1980, between Ronald Reagan and Jimmy Carter. The one where I voted wrong. I didn't often hear my dad's opinion on politics in general. He mostly avoided it; and besides, he got all of his opinions from the Bible.

The Bible was …well, the Bible in our house. The Word. The Word of God. It was the inspired, Holy scripture.

Mom and Dad gave me my first Bible when I "got saved," at 8 years old, and I began reading my Bible daily.

In 1984, thinking that we had been gifted mysteriously with a beautiful King James Version Bible, my sisters and I began celebrating. God had sent us a Bible!! We had no idea how or why, but we were sure that He sent it. A Bible was the most precious gift that we knew of! Now who were we supposed to give it to?

Uncle Steve!!

We all agreed instantly that Uncle Steve was the guy.

Imagine our chagrin when one of us happened to open the flap and see all of my family information and the dedication that my folks had written to me in the front of...... my own Bible. A church that we had just visited had sent it to me immediately upon finding it left behind.

We were so bummed that it was not a Bible that we could send to Steve!! We recovered quickly, as kids do sometimes. One of us had a brilliant idea; what if we all pooled our money and BOUGHT a new Bible for Uncle Steve?!!

This idea had become such a thing of joy, that before Mom got home from work we were already sure that we had enough to buy one. All of our pennies, nickels, dimes, quarters, a couple dollar bills, along with assorted hair-bands and other pre-teen valuables were scattered in a rough pile on the kitchen table. We had no idea what the cost of a brand new Bible might be, but surely with ALL of our money......

My sisters asked me if we had enough, and I, putting on my shrewdest, almost-11-face guessed that we did. Mom, when she got home from work, was kind enough not to burst our bubble. I am sure we were probably far short, and she was barely making enough to pay the household bills.

Dad was very sick every day with migraines. Really bad migraines. We could not go into the bedroom to disturb him, for the most part - other than washing his head with a hot cloth for hours, because it would help his pain a little. I hated that he had headaches; it looked awful on his face. Sometimes he turned almost green.

He slowly got better, but back then he was in bed much of the time.

In spite of Dad's health, my mother somehow scraped enough together and made sure that we sent Uncle Steve that Bible. I was not sure that he was as grateful as we thought he would be, but I knew that he was always very kind and fun to be around, so I figured that he understood the love behind it, even if he never decided to become much of a Bible reader.

I was. I read it cover-to-cover, many times, because it was very important to Dad, and I admired my dad greatly. My dad was definitely a man of God. Dad once fasted and prayed for 21 days. No food, just water, like Elijah, or Daniel. I was in awe; I fasted for three days once and I hated it. I couldn't imagine 21 days! The worst thing was, on the 22nd day, when he "broke" his fast, he was so hungry that he ate a beef steak. In the next hours and days, we thought that he might die. He did not know that the human stomach cannot simply go from eating nothing to eating a 20 oz. beef steak without causing major digestion problems.

We all learned that when you fast, even for three days, you had better come off of it slow and easy. Fasting would become an important part of our "spiritual walk"

Honor thy Father and thy Mother.

"Honor thy father and thy mother: that thy days may be long upon the land that the Lord thy God giveth thee." Exodus 20:12

In our family, when one was re-writing a scripture verse it was very important to get it exactly right. Every single "jot and tittle" must be exactly right. Otherwise it was a sin. There is a verse about the jot and the tittle, and another one about how it is a sin to misrepresent the Word of God. Dad always put the highest emphasis on the Bible, especially the King James Version. To this day, it is like a filter that I see the world through; or, you could say that I see the world through my parent's interpretation of the Holy Book.

That verse about your parents is the first of the Ten Commandments "with promise;" meaning that the Commandments before it only told you what "Thou shalt not" do, but this one said what *to do*, and promised a blessing if you did it. In my family, we believed in this blessing whole-heartedly. We extended this verse to mean that if you disobeyed your parents, you would be cursed.

In practice, for the Carpenter family, that meant that my parents would tell me what was right and wrong for my life. And, should I disobey their direction for my life, it was the same thing as disobeying God. Disobeying God carried massive consequences.

In our faith, it was a requirement to get saved. No one would get into heaven, the promised after-life of celebration and ease, unless one was saved. And being saved, according to the Bible and the people who interpreted it for me, meant having an experience of repentance, confessing my sins, and asking Jesus to come into my heart.

He would then wash my sins away, through the legal authority that He earned by dying on the Cross in my place, (and the place of all sinners) at Calvary, on a hill in Jerusalem. The alternative was to pay the price for my sins myself, through eternal torment in Hell, a literal lake of fire. There, a person would burn eternally without relief, and be separated from God - down there with Satan and the Demons. This is what we believed. There were a few different prayers that people recommended for getting saved, and everyone that I knew (for the most part) agreed that you must be saved. I definitely wanted to go to heaven.

In short, if you were *not* saved, you would go to hell, and if you *were* saved, you would go to heaven.

Faced with a choice between those two extremes, it seemed very important to me to be saved. My Grandpa Bob, whom I adored, had a slightly different view, one that he may have concocted himself. He used to say that you make your own heaven and your own hell. Right here. Right now.

I was not ready to take the chance that he could be right. So one day, at age 8, and deeply convicted of my sins, I prayed the prayer under the stairs at the house in Littlefork. I had heard of a beautiful feeling of peace that one should have when one gets saved - but I honestly felt nothing different. I prayed under a feeling of heavy conviction, but after confessing and asking forgiveness and "accepting Jesus into my heart," I felt even more pressure to be good and perform. And some confusion about what I should be doing next; but at least I was saved, so that was a relief.

My mom often got compliments when we attended church about how we kids sat quietly all the way through the service, hands folded, four heads looking politely ahead at the pastor, apparently rapt attention being given to what might be a dry sermon - especially for an 8-year-old, or even a 4-year-old.

We were learning to control ourselves, to be respectful, to be quiet when necessary. These are great skills. But, for better or worse, we were learning to modify our behavior in order to please God; and pleasing God was defined by our parents and their interpretation of the Bible.

We were also beginning to learn another lesson that we practiced heavily for the next decade. We were learning how to fake it.

"Wherefore come out from among them, and be ye separate, saith the Lord, and touch not the unclean thing, and I will receive you." 2 Corinthians 6:17

My Dad had a very vivid dream one night when I was about 5, and I heard the story many times in my life. During the dream, the above verse was impressed upon him. He quoted this verse anytime he wanted to illustrate why we were different.

We did not conform to "the world" so that we would not be "partakers of her plagues" (another verse). This teaching came to mean to me that we would not do what most people did. We always did the unusual, we always stayed partly aloof from others. When our Gospel Music career ended, the 10,000 people on our mailing list that felt that they were our fans and our friends were deeply hurt and surprised that they never heard another thing from any of us. They did not understand that even while we were being friendly with them at concerts, we had a basic belief that we needed to maintain an internal separation from "the world."

If you were not a family member, you were "the world." No one on the outside would know the real us. We would not partake of her plagues. We were better than that; better than them. Smarter, holier, more prepared; God's special people. No one who is still in the family cult today would say it this way, but it is how they live, and what I lived for several decades.

Dad truly believed that the world was going to be wiped out, and that our only hope was to be separate from it. Growing up, we were, indeed, very separate. Our few friends tended to be outside the mainstream, as well. The Pearson Family were Jehovah's Witnesses. For a while, in 1980-81, we lived with the Hege Family, who were Mennonite. We had regular visits from a Seventh-Day Adventist couple, Leonard and Cathy Lang. Dad even brought home a hippy couple one time; the man had long hair and their son was called Moon Child and his teeth were rotten at age four because he drank nothing but horse's milk.

Mom just shook her head, because these early family relationships of ours were really Dad's friends. Mom's friends would have been very mainstream, very "worldly," and probably would have thought that we were nuts, watching our odd lifestyle.

My dad spent many hours with these unusual friends of his, debating and learning what they believed, based on his understanding of the Bible. He and his friends shared the impression that we were all outsiders. He slowly formulated a doctrine that we lived by, and it seemed to incorporate various things that he read or liked about some of these early friends' beliefs.

My Mom clearly loved my Dad deeply in those early days, because her heart wanted to be successful ("normal" she would say back then). We all knew that we were very much not normal, and that it was, in fact, an intentional part of Dad's beliefs. And Mom always adhered firmly to what he said, even if she grumbled. In order to stay "separate," we kids had very few friends in the traditional sense of the word, and grew up being each other's best friends.

An early addict to television, Dad "threw out the TV" when I was 1-year-old, and he did not have a TV in the house again until I was 17; even then, it was just for carefully censored movies.

We were each home-schooled through our senior year.

My sisters wore a lot of dresses.

We never swore. My sister, Sarah, literally thought that the "F word" was "fart" until she was in her 20's. We said toot.

Friends were very carefully monitored, and love interests were even more intently censored.

Until after I left home, the Carpenter family did not celebrate Christmas - at all; it was too commercial.

Or Halloween.

No bikinis, or any revealing clothing for girls.

No sex before marriage. I did not know what sex was, but I was very clear that it was for after marriage, so, until marriage, I did not need to know about it.

No alcohol. I knew what alcohol was; Mom had been very traumatized by Grandpa Bob's drinking, and she was very clear with us that it was evil. When I was 8 or 9 she had to get a can of beer to kill the slugs in the garden, and she let me taste it. It was awful. She told me to always stay away from it. Until I left home, I did stay away from it, and never have particularly loved beer.

No social security numbers for us kids. There are passages in the Book of Revelations that talk about the "Mark of the Beast" which is a number, and, according to the scriptures, at the "end times," or end of the world, one will not be able to buy or sell without the number. Dad is convinced that the Social Security System was designed to introduce a number that you would need to buy or sell. "It is the Mark of the Beast System!" he would intone ominously. Until I finally received my social security number, around age 19, I learned that it was indeed very difficult to buy, sell, or earn money without one.

Before I was 10, we kids had very little contact with friends outside of each other. Mom told me that I had an imaginary friend named Blossom, and I held the door and set out chairs for Blossom until Blossom disappeared when I was about five. Since Dad was home-schooling us in order to "keep us separate," it didn't make sense for us to be allowed to play with just anybody.

My first "normal" friendship was struck up with a loud, tall, gangly fellow-ten-year-old at Sand Hill Lake Bible Camp. My parents, craving connection with like-minded people, decided to take a chance on a church-based Bible Camp that my Uncle Bob and his wife, Marcie, were attending. It was near us too, so travel costs would not be prohibitive.

My new camp friend's name was Kenneth Donald Luebeck, and he was called Kenny. We loved intellectual discussions, and with his thick glasses and odd speech, he was very much an outsider - like me. We got into a very heated debate with a couple of older girls at Sand Hill Lake, defending the idea of Creation vs Evolution. We were both passionate about our beliefs, and even though the girls were probably just trying to get some boy attention, we argued with fervor and intelligence.

Kenny and I were kind to each other. He didn't raise waves with my parents, and I didn't make fun of his mannerisms. He eventually grew out of the odd mannerisms and we continue to be friends to this day.

When we said "good-bye," at Camp, we exchanged addresses and I did not expect that I would ever see him again. He lived in Ramsey, Minnesota, and I had no idea where in the universe that might be. We wrote letters, but neither of us loved writing, so that tapered off after a while.

In the months following Camp, my Dad felt that God was telling him to "Broaden our horizons," so he took a job selling Watkins products, door-to-door. Mom and Dad decided to leave International Falls, Minnesota. They spent many evenings walking around the school in the Falls and talking about this big decision while we kids played at the playground. They were scared to death because the Falls was all that they knew. The decision to leave "Up North" took us, ultimately, to Eden Road. At the time that we first left the Falls, however, I hated it. This "Broadening our horizons" was so unpredictable, uncomfortable, and scary.

In our travels, and in our poverty, we ended up needing friends. After a few months of hard experiences out on the road, broke, hungry, and in need of showers, we journeyed to the church where my Uncle Bob was an Assistant Pastor. It was called Faith Fellowship, in Elk River, Minnesota. The Watkins business had been very hard on our finances, and our emotions. We kids were selling door-to-door too, for food every day, and our rental at the time had no working water. The water it did have smelled very strongly of sulphur, and all of us, even Mom, had to bathe in the creek in order to do the Watkins parties that were critical to our sales and survival.

I hated this; we felt very, very poor, and nothing was remotely similar to what we had known Up North. It felt embarrassing to me that we were constantly relying on the kindness of someone else to get basic necessities, like a shower or food. I could tell that Mom was humiliated by it as well. We moved constantly, and nothing was secure.

It was 1985; I had turned 11, and I was miserable. Mom was concerned for my emotional health, and in all of the upheaval of puberty that was to come, it was the last time I would feel that concern from her.

Our family's needs caused our facade of independence and "separateness" to crumble for a couple of years, and we found that people were unbelievably kind. The people at Faith Fellowship took us in, gave us showers, and food; Tim and Becky West, transplants from Wyoming, offered for Dad to go to work with Tim as a trim carpenter. Tim and Becky West are still considered our family's best friends to this day. Partnering with Tim was the most financially sound decision that Dad had made, and our finances improved.

Terry Seaborg and Nancy Cato, a couple of single ladies in the church offered us a house to live in, in exchange for Dad's construction help on the property. It was unbelievable. Terry and Nancy became dear friends as well.

As we walked into the worship service that first Sunday morning at Faith Fellowship, everyone was being so nice, and we were being cared for! My mom was happy, and she had not been happy for quite a while. I was very in-tune with her emotions.

And then, I almost stopped dead in my tracks. On our way to the pew, I saw him. Arms akimbo, clapping along to the worship song in his trademark fashion, in the third row on the left, was Kenny Luebeck!! Faith Fellowship just happened to be his family's church. These seats were his family's permanent home.

It would mark the deepening of a life-long friendship, and would be a much-needed social experience that I had been starving for. Ken Luebeck would prove to be a really great friend. We both loved model railroads, the Bible, and learning obscure details. We both excelled in class, he at Elk River High School, and I at our Home-school.

Dad and Mom moved us to Elk River, and settled into a more "normal" lifestyle for a time, going to church at Faith Fellowship for the next two years. Mom loved it, and we kids were so happy to have money and friends! After the barren wasteland of Watkins sales and rotten-smelling rentals, or the isolation of the woods Up North, this was the Promised Land.

Ken's best friend at church had been Stephanie Deutchmann, and she and my next younger sister, Leah, became friends. The four of us became inseparable. We were in the same Sunday School group, and Steph, Kenny, and I loved theological discussions. Leah went along for the social events, but didn't love the theory and debates.

One night after church, Stephanie was having an issue of some kind, and I sensed that she was in need of help somehow. She and I ended up on the back stairs of the church, talking. I was very concerned for her emotions. Looking back, I think there was a lot more going on than I could process from my very theoretical headspace. I felt that I was being a good friend.

I must have been at least a little interested in Stephanie for more than intellectual purposes that night on the staircase at Faith, because I was happy to be alone with her. She may have been hoping for something more in the way of a physical connection, but I was oblivious to that if she was.

My Uncle Bob, as an Assistant Pastor at Faith Fellowship, went hustling by doing errands around the church, taking the stairs three at a time. I remember the surprise on his face as he saw me chatting alone on the back staircase with a girl. He mentioned something about seeing me and Steph to my mom, who later grilled me. I had nothing to deny, and I was very much a truth-teller at that time. So she rested assured that I was just mildly interested. But I was warned about being alone with girls.

My family, the Wests, Uncle Bob's family, and Kenny's family were among the last to leave any church function, and all of us loved the fellowship and fun that we shared during those times.

While our parents socialized inside, Kenny and I and the other young people would run around on the huge church lawn, getting into mischief, racing each other, and talking endlessly about whatever came to our minds. On one such Sunday evening, not that many weeks after my stairwell discussion with Stephanie, Kenny broached a subject to me that he seemed to be quite interested in.

It felt like he was trying to determine what I knew, and he was being very cryptic.

"Come on!" I said, often exasperated with Ken's careful fact-building and back-story, "Just spit it out! Spell it if you have to!"

"S," he said, looking sharply for recognition in my eyes. Nothing.

"E." Still nothing. He pushed his glasses up and squinted his eyes in his trademark fashion, looking sidelong at me.

"X."

I had heard of the word, but it meant absolutely nothing to me. He could see it on my face.

Ken was always very kind, and no matter what he already knew about S-E-X, he respected my innocence that night.

"Forget it," he muttered, "it's not a big deal."

I considered asking my mom about it, but decided against it. It didn't seem like something that she would want to talk about, so I decided that whatever it was, it wasn't important.

At home, we were becoming little adults. Washing dishes, cleaning the house, taking out the trash, and feeding pets became proving grounds for our abilities to be responsible and mature. I struggled with that. Getting the dishes clean enough was a challenge for my random, 12-year-old brain, and Mom became exasperated with me. One plate that was not washed properly was broken over my head.

The next time that Mom discovered a badly washed dish of mine, she came up behind me and grabbed me by the short hair at the back of my scalp. As she yelled at me, she jerked repeatedly on that hair. It was really painful, and with her last declaration it came out in her fingers - all that she had grabbed came out, leaving a bald spot. I thought little of it, other than to try harder to clean all of the dishes properly, and laughingly showed people at church my bald spot. I was not prepared for her anger when we got home. I was soundly chewed out for telling people what she did, and as much as she valued honesty, this was the first time that I realized that it didn't apply to her.

Towards the end of those two years in Elk River, at age 13, I discovered that my sheets felt really good on a certain part of me. The first time it happened, I was shocked because it was feeling SO good, and then suddenly I lost control and peed the bed. I got up to clean up the mess, shocked and embarrassed that I had peed the bed at age 13. Truth be told, I had a bed-wetting problem until age 10, so I ashamedly just decided to clean it up and not tell Mom. That was when I realized that it wasn't pee. It was weird and white. I could not figure it out. It was hard to wash out as well, not like pee. I would never ask Mom about it; she had ridiculed me for peeing the bed when I was younger, so I would not take that risk with this weird thing.

But it felt so good, that I would soon be doing it again.

Chapter 4
Eden Road

There is a story about two children, each given a crate for their birthday.

The first child opened his crate and saw a Shetland pony, but immediately began to worry that he didn't know how to care for a pony, and ended up crying inconsolably because he was sure that the pony would die. The second child opened his crate, and found it to be full to the top with stinking horse manure. He gleefully shouted, "Oh boy, there must be a pony in here somewhere and I bet I can get a bunch of money for this fertilizer!" as he ran for the wheelbarrow to start loading it up.

Heaven is what you make it.

I was 13, in 1987, when we moved out to the farm in Morgan, Minnesota, on Eden Road.

It was here that my parents would create their own version of Eden; their little piece of heaven, and they would work very hard ideologically, economically, and politically to keep "the World" out - and their prized possessions (and me and my siblings) in.

Mom and Dad, together with us older kids, created the Carpenter Family "cult," according to the definition of that word. We made decisions as a group, and we were directed primarily by my mother on the day to day. My father judged what was right and wrong for everyone, based upon his interpretation of scripture. He was very hardline on some things, but very lax on others.

The only people that really mattered in our world were the cult members. We were in or out, based upon our compliance. If, as a member, you chose to disagree with the leaders of the group (Mom or Dad), the rest of the group would turn on you to convince, manipulate, or force you to agree. If you did not comply, you would be shunned from the group. The cult's jurisdiction extended over the individual's finances, dating life, values (especially values!) and even the cult's highest stated value, one's relationship with God.

We learned how the politics of this cult worked during Gripe Nights.

Mom had instituted "Gripe Night" during the late 80's and early 90's, putting the name to it in 1988 when we had as many as five extra boys in our home or home-school. Mom was just starting the adoptions, so it seemed like chaos - and extra children - were the norm. Each of us (there were 10 of us on average, with Mom and Dad) would go around the room and say if we had a problem with anyone else in the group; it served to clear the air, and get stuff out in the open.

It sounds good on the face of it, maybe, but it turned into ganging up, with Mom's blessing and usually under her direction, on whomever was in the "Hot-seat" that night. It was a chance to "correct" any wrong-thinking by an individual and distill our group-rule. We had christened one particular chair in the living room "the Hot-seat" because it seemed that whoever was about to get called out would happen to be sitting in that chair for Gripe Night.

On one evening, however, Gripe Night backfired, because Mom lost control, and she was the one in "the Hot-seat." She argued. She defended. She used all of the tricks that she had taught us to recognize as excuses. But we kids were growing in strength and numbers, and we would not let her off of the hook. We were "holding her accountable" the way we did each other. So she threw herself on the floor and started kicking and screaming.

Literally.

She kicked so violently that she broke the ornate wooden leg off of the antique, parlor-style chair that my sister Sarah was sitting in. Sarah toppled to the floor, and we all rushed in to console Mom, who lay on the floor sobbing. Dad ran in to console her as well. She asked for the little kids, who were sleeping at the time, and we pulled them from their cribs and brought them to her. They were just babies, and for some reason she wanted to hold all three of them. The issue that we were addressing with her was forgotten in the drama, and we were all aware of a new and deep fear.

We all now realized that if we crossed her, she might crack. Gripe Night, and our mob rule, would never apply to her.

In the outside world, the Minnesota Twins were headed to the World Series that fall, and the Iran Contra Affair dominated headlines. The U. S. President Ronald Reagan underwent surgery for prostate cancer, bringing up questions about his ability to govern. *Teenage Mutant Ninja Turtles, Married With Children,* and *Beauty and the Beast* were on the screens, and *Fatal Attraction, Lethal Weapon,* and *Dirty Dancing* were instant classics. There were a large number of popular movies from that era; *Predator, Throw Momma From the Train,* and *The Princess Bride* are just a few more.

I would see none of these iconic films - or even really know much about them until much later in life. We still did not own a TV, and the only current events that we would have access to were through WCCO Radio, out of the Twin Cities. On WCCO, we would hear talk radio, and I also got to follow the final half of the Minnesota Twins' season - mostly from the cab of a tractor as I did farm work in our township. The whole family was glued to the radio in October when the Minnesota Twins won their first World Series since 1924.

My days were filled with nothing complicated. I worked for neighboring farmers, wrote piano pieces, did my home schooling, and spent many hours reading and working on my model railroad. We were all relieved to not be moving every year or two; it felt like we were home, and we had plenty of room to enjoy the simple things on our little 5-acre farm on Eden Road.

One autumn evening in Eden Township, a herd of cows belonging to one of our neighbors got out of the fence near our house. This was when we older kids were in our late teens. We knew whose cows they were, but it was pitch black outside. Since most of the cows were coal-black, we started trying to round them up right away. If someone came flying down the road and hit one, we would all feel responsible. We chased those cows for hours. I will never forget my sister, Sarah, herding one cow into a corner of the fence, while others of us chased the rest. This one cow could not be seen very well, but Sarah could hear it breathing, so she just blocked it from getting out onto the road. Imagine her surprise when the early morning light revealed that she had been holding the big bull captive for hours!

That's how it was growing up. People bravely and simply took care of each other. When my little sister, Susanna (our second adopted sibling), was three months old and flying home with Mom from Belize, we older kids could scarcely contain our excitement. We counted the days until they touched down at the Minneapolis/St. Paul Airport. We cleaned the house spotlessly to impress Mom when she got back.

The night of their flight up through Houston, Texas, from Belize, there was a terrible blizzard in Minnesota. Terry Seaborg, our dear friend who was supposed to drive the 100 miles out to the farm and get us teens, could not even attempt the run in the snow, as she had a very small car. We cried because we were so disappointed to miss out on Susanna's entry to the US and to our family.

Tim West, my dad's work partner, who was working near Mankato, Minnesota, heard about our ride falling through. He knew in his heart how crushed we would be; so after work, in his big work van, he and Becky made the trip out to get us. After delivering us, in time, to the airport (safe and sound and so grateful!) he had to drive another two hours in the drifting snow, back to work early the next morning. He must have slept for less than four hours that night. I will never forget his kindness to four farm kids who just wanted to hold their new baby sister as soon as humanly possible. I loved that man. He was the example of God's love for us that night.

We kids were invited to join the Eden Eagles, the 4-H organization in Eden township. We attended some events, and got to know our neighbors, but that was about all. We met some great kids, and became quick friends, but they were "too worldly" for my dad, and so even though we might invite them over to the farm, we were not allowed to get involved in anything that would take us off of our farm and Mom's watchful eye. It was beginning to be apparent that I thought some of the neighbor girls were cute, and they reciprocated. Mom monitored that very carefully.

We *were* allowed to go to the neighboring farms for one thing, however: work. Because we did not have Social Security Numbers, the only way we could make any money was to work for "cash on the side." And the news began to spread that we were exceptional workers. Most of the neighbors would eventually hire us at one time or another. Some balked at not "claiming" the money on their taxes, but for most, the work we did was so good that it was worth a slightly illegal financial transaction. Many farmers shared my dad's mistrust of the Government, though I don't think any of them shared his fear of the "Mark of the Beast." I think their willingness to thwart the system had more to do with avoiding payroll taxes and liability.

It was a cool, wet morning that was just starting to dry into a hot, humid afternoon in the soybean field where we were "walking beans" when Mom and Dad pulled up to the far end of the rows where we were walking. Fields were often a quarter-mile and more in length, so from our end of the lush, green soybean field the big family van looked tiny in the cloud of dust that followed it on the little gravel farm road.

A short footnote on "bean-walking:" before there were poisons to kill specific weeds, farmers in our part of Minnesota and around the country would hire local kids to walk through the fields with a hoe (a long-handled right-angle cutting tool) and the crew would pull or chop out any of the weeds that could be found.

It was hard work, and we Carpenter kids had up to seven different farmers that would hire us to walk their fields every summer. We occasionally worked with "town kids" from nearby Morgan, and on those days there may be as many as 11 or 12 kids walking through the field. With that many young people in one field, there would be much horseplay, girl-chasing, boy-chasing, and general mischief of all kinds. As much fun as the "town kids" were, however, they were usually not very good at the job, and we had to clean up after them. Mom and Dad didn't like it when we walked with the town kids. They seemed to not trust them. Consequently, we four kids often walked with just the farmer. Mom and Dad would help clean fields in later years - when we were so trusted that the farmers would simply point us to a field and let us clean it on our own and turn in our hours for pay. We made $4-$6 per hour. It was grueling work, but peaceful.

On a typical bean-walking day, at some time around 5:30 am, whichever farmer we were working for would pull up to the house, and we would all pile into the back of his pick-up for the very chilly ride in the early morning darkness to whatever field we were cleaning up that day. The farmers knew exactly when the sunrise was, so the dark, cold drive ended at the edge of the field just as the sun came up. We would pile out in our hooded sweatshirts, each with our favorite wooden-handled hoe, to start walking. I hated the feeling of soaked jeans sticking to my legs, and early morning was the coldest and wettest. Even when it had not rained, the dew in southern Minnesota collected on the velvety soybean leaves and, as I brushed by them, soaked my jeans from the knees down in a matter of a few strides.

As we started our first "round" to the end of the field and back, the farmer would decide how many rows would be between each "walker." That number was completely determined by two things: crop height (how easy it was to see over each row) and how "dirty" the field was. If he said, "Let's take two rows each," we knew he was expecting a very weedy field. As we walked, we pulled or chopped each weed out, and hopped across rows to help each other out if it happened to be weedier in someone else's row. On days when the farmer gave us five or even six rows between, we would be mostly walking fast and getting a few small weeds, reflecting a very "clean" field. The better a field was cleaned year after year, the fewer weed seeds there would be to scatter on the fall wind, and the cleaner the field would be the following years. Conversely, if one of our regular farmer employers bought a new field that had not been walked correctly in years, it was sure to be extremely weedy.

Back to that day in 1988 when we saw the big, green Ford Econoline van rolling up to the end of the rows. As we hurriedly cleaned the long rows to the other end, we chattered excitedly amongst ourselves, because Mom and Dad very rarely showed up to where we were working. When we got to the end, we took a water break.

Mom and Dad had news indeed. We were being asked to come and perform our music at yet another local venue. What had started at a church for Mother's Day, singing at the request of a home-schooler friend, was snowballing into an actual gig schedule.

This time, they wanted to PAY us. They wanted to pay us $50. We were so excited, we could hardly stand it.

But there was a catch.

We stopped jumping and doing weird gymnastics with our hoes to note the serious tone. Mom said, "They don't have a piano."

What?!! This was cruel! A disaster.

Our group sound was built around my piano playing, and my sisters' singing. Leah's guitar was a nice addition, but it was not something we had practiced with like we had with the piano. This was a real problem. But Mom and Dad had a solution. And in this solution was born a whole lot of dreams, and just as many terrible fights.

"IF," Mom said, and she emphasized the pause..... "IF you want to, you could all pool your money, and we could look at getting a keyboard for Joshua."

Our mouths dropped. She went on, slipping Dad a sidelong smile that said they had already discussed this at length, "Me and Dad would buy it now, and you guys would pay us back out of your earnings this summer."

I could not believe my ears. I had wanted an electronic keyboard for a while now, because it would be portable. We could play anywhere!! But at 4.25/hour for walking beans, it would take me a couple of summers to pay it off on my own.

We looked at each other, and there was a minimum of discussion. "So we could get this for the gig this weekend?" someone asked.

"Yep!" Dad was grinning from ear to ear. "And you could put the $50 from the gig towards the new keyboard too!"

I was 14; Leah, 13; Sarah, 11, and Melita, 10. We were all in. You could feel it immediately. There was no dragging of feet, or argument.

"YES!" Somebody said it out loud.

I thrilled at being allowed to leave the field, and go shopping that day for a keyboard - with money that Mom and Dad fronted us and that my sisters had just committed to paying off with me.

And from then on that was how the Carpenter Family Singers worked.

We all pooled our money, and Mom managed it. Our first PA system. An equipment trailer to pull behind the family van. Bigger PA systems. A school bus with a trailer. A full Greyhound tour bus. Two of them. Posters, Cassettes. Compact Discs. We financed it all as a group, using money that we made walking beans, chasing turkeys, driving tractor, cleaning houses, mowing lawns, and performing shows. Mom and Dad repeatedly took out mortgages against the farm to pay up front, and then we all hustled like mad, often working three jobs each to pay it off. It was amazing. And it was destined to fall.

The Farm on Eden Road, later named *The House of Lights* by my mother, became my parents' little utopia. The Farm, and the extension of it that became the Carpenter Family Singers was not in fact, Heaven. It was an Empire, and Mom and Dad were the legal, political, and fiscal owners.

Chapter 5   Dad

My Dad, Michael Bruce Carpenter was 6'2" tall, with very kind blue eyes, and a full head of curly, dark brown hair. He has naturally lighter skin tones, although he has been told that he has Native American blood in his heritage.

Dad had an extremely abusive early childhood, until he was adopted. His biological dad used to kick and beat him, and his birth mom had to walk into rooms backwards because she could not mentally face what was inside. Until he was 8, Little Dad was regularly left in a remote cabin near Blackduck, Minnesota, foraging and cooking food for himself and Rick.

Dad was adopted at the age of 8, along with his little brother, Rick, age 6. They were adopted by an elderly couple from International Falls, Minnesota - my Grandpa and Grandma Carpenter, Howard and Eula, who had lost their only son, Jerry, to one of those diseases that people died of back in the day. Grandpa and Grandma Carpenter were in their 50's when they adopted the boys, and in their 70's by the time that I came along.

Grandpa Carpenter planned carefully for his adopted sons' college, and invested in several different insurance plans and retirements to care for his loved ones when he passed.

After Dad graduated high-school and Mom and Dad got married, Grandpa Carpenter paid for Dad to go to college in Bemidji, Minnesota, to be a teacher like my Grandma Carpenter, his adopted mom. Grandpa Carpenter was an Electrical Inspector for the State of Minnesota, working out of International Falls. He and Grandma Carpenter loved my mom to death.

My mom wanted to attend college with Dad, but I was conceived instead, and she supported Dad and raised me instead of achieving any of her career dreams. It was the culture of her time. She would tell me later that she really had wanted to test her abilities in a career, and regretted her decision not to pursue higher education. She was also somewhat resentful that Dad had his college paid for.

Dad was very quiet in a large group, though he had strong opinions if asked. He could get very passionate and forceful about any subject that he cared about, and forget himself in the discussion, getting louder and more insistent as he talked.

Dad was so likable; he was a dead shot, and he loved hunting, fishing, and raising animals. He also loved gardening, and woods lore. But his favorite thing in the world was to kick back in his La-Z-Boy recliner and talk about intellectual things.

He loved topics like the Book of Revelation in the Bible, or how his latest construction project would help protect our family from the coming Apocalypse.

Dad had a charming, quiet way of hearing you and noticing things that others dismiss. He was the master of not saying everything that he was thinking, letting his kids learn things for themselves, quietly noticing if we were in danger, but choosing to let us have our own experience as long as we were not going to die. He seemed to just *know* when there was no point in telling me something. He could tell when I had made up my mind, and would need to discover the truth or danger for myself.

My dad accepted everyone, including random strangers exactly as they were. He could chat and be kind to anyone, regardless of their station in life. In fact, he felt more comfortable with a homeless Rastafarian on the streets of Belize City than he did with the Governor of his home State of Minnesota, USA. He has stories about both of those interactions.

Dad was not long on talk when it came to his convictions. He loved to repeat them to his children and wife, but with the public, he preferred action over talking. If they thought he wouldn't do it, he would. He did not care about the cost, being willing to take any extreme measure if he believed that it was the right way to do it. He was a true rebel and he always had a cause.

Dad was amazing, and he had some flaws that I knew of; he was emotionally distant, he tended to use people, and he had an addictive personality.

Possibly because of his childhood pain, Dad liked to focus on activities, and ideas, instead of connecting emotionally. I loved him to death, and, in order to really get close to him I learned that I needed to help him with a project. He would not sit down with me and ask me about my heart. It was not bad, it just was. He talked and laughed and connected while he worked.

One of the things that bothered me the most after I left home was the realization that I had been used by my dad, with Mom's help.

When I was 13 and we had just moved out to the Farm, Dad wanted to get goats again. Mom hated them. She constantly reminded him that during one of her pregnancies, he had 27 brush-goats that he fed - but she was not allowed to use the electric blanket for her legs because it would cost too much. This memory consistently came up as a testimony to the fact that he did not really love her. But he talked her into getting one purebred Saanen again, at Eden Road, for milk. Saanen is the breed that gives the most milk.

Dad turned to me. This was before the music business had started, and before we were running all of our finances through Mom. I had saved some cash from my rock-picking and farm work.

"Maybe you want to go into this with me?" he asked.

"Really?" I was surprised. I had no interest, honestly.

He knew that I was into my model railroad. I had been eyeing several cool additions to my set, which took up half of my bedroom. But he didn't really understand my fixation with tiny, working models.

I realized, however, that it would be a way to impress him.... it felt to me like an invitation to be an adult.

He wasn't into my train-set anyway. It was kind of dumb.

"At least a goat would have some practical value!" Mom encouraged. She saw little value in the trains either.

"Okay!" I agreed.

It took all of my money to buy a second goat, Missy, that was available for purchase from the same farm as Dad's goat, named Treasure. This started our herd. It was years, even after I left home, before I realized that Dad had created not only the purchase price of the extra goat using all of my cash, but guess who was now responsible for half of the milking chores? It was my goat after all! This is just one example of Dad's pattern.

I had watched this pattern with my Grandpa Carpenter, the electrical inspector who was my inspiration for becoming an electrician. As Grandpa aged and began to fail, I had the feeling that Dad seemed to be waiting, maybe with anticipation even, for Grandpa Carpenter to die, because he was certain that he would get a large inheritance. Mom and Dad discussed it often as Grandpa aged, and more after Grandma Carpenter passed away.

They were incensed when Grandpa remarried very late in life, and furious that he spent a lot of money on his new wife, a long-time friend of the family. I did not feel that my dad was all that connected to Grandpa emotionally, but then, I don't think he connected to anyone that way.

My parents hid their anger and greed from anyone outside the family, and when they found the farm at Eden Road, Grandpa Carpenter wrote Mom and Dad a check for $30,000 to pay for the first two thirds of the $45,000 purchase price.

Dad paid the last $15,000 by keeping his job in the Twin Cities with Tim West for ten more months. Dad slept in the condos he was trimming during the week, and returned the 100 miles to the Farm each weekend. When the Farm was paid off, he looked for a job in our area, eventually starting at Kraft Foods, in nearby New Ulm, Minnesota.

Dad's pay and benefits from his Kraft Foods job made the house payment (we almost always had a mortgage against it for something, even after we paid it off the first time) and took care of the minor children's medical care. We would not have been able to operate the music business and keep the property had Dad not been willing to stay home and take care of those things, especially in the early years when the music business was sucking up every bit of cash that any of us made. With the family out on the road touring, often for months, it seemed that his and Mom's relationship enjoyed the space. There was no love lost between them at that point in their marriage, and I was unwittingly replacing her need for a male partner, emotionally.

I gave my parents' sex lives not a second thought, though at one point in my mother's "accountability" help, she told me that she had sold the Jacuzzi tub because she found herself making the wrong use of it. I think she was trying to make me feel less shame about my own masturbation, but I didn't want to hear or even think about hers. Dad and Mom went months without seeing each other, and it was often confrontational when they did, so I can't imagine that their love life could have been awesome. It was the last thing that I wanted to think about then.

My dad had a very addictive personality. He collected everything, and anything that he saw value in. Children. Animals. Partially used beehives, an old cream separator, many gardening and farming tools and hand-cranked equipment. I think he justified the collecting because of his constant fear and belief that, "The system is going to crash someday!"

I grew up totally fearing this event, and spent many hours plotting with my dad to prepare for it. We were original preppers, but not smart or cool like some that I see now on TV. For my Dad, there was a high level of fear, interspersed with maybe even a little glee at the idea of going back to pre-electricity days. He always felt that the 50's were the golden age, and he longed for the simpler times of yore. At the same time, Dad was not prepared to give up the comfort and convenience that things like cars and refrigerators afforded. One of his favorite books at that time was *"Henry and the Great Society,"* about a man who trades his quiet, hardscrabble farm life for a factory job and all of the finer things, only to have a personal crisis around whether any of the "progress" that he had experienced was actually good. I won't spoil the book for you, because it is worth reading. My dad felt that book deeply.

Y2K

It was December of 1999. Jay-Z stabbed record executive Lance "Un" Rivera at a nightclub in New York City; *Deuce Bigalow; Girl, Interrupted;* and *The Green Mile* were out on the big screen. Internationally, France was seeing epic storms that took down their power grid, the United Kingdom was giving control of Northern Ireland to the Northern Ireland Executive, and on the 31st, New Year's Eve, control of the Panama Canal would pass from the United States back to Panama. At the same time, New Year's Eve, 2000, the computers that our economy and infrastructure now relied on were expected to suffer an unforeseen and unavoidable world-wide glitch. Entire systems and nations were expected to fail. The whole world had finally begun to talk like Dad had been for years.

And Dad was on high alert. He had found a good deal at Cash Wise Foods on two things: tuna fish and toilet paper. It was his joy to shop for deals every night on his way home from the Kraft Foods factory where he worked as a cook making Velveeta Cheese. In order to prepare for the coming Apocalypse he bought 500 cans of tuna and hundreds of rolls of toilet paper. We stacked them in the partially-built Music Studio, a 2400 square foot building that was not completed while I was at home. The tuna and toilet paper sat there for years, and the tuna, they tell me, eventually went bad. They couldn't even feed it to the cats.

Those are the kind of odd things that my Dad did. Still does, from what I understand. The reality of Y2K was decidedly a non-event for the world, and The Carpenter Family Singers celebrated the New Year in a condo with a pool on South Padre Island, and had a blast. We were secure knowing that if things went bad, we could drive the bus 1500 miles back to Eden Road in Morgan, Minnesota and get our tuna and toilet paper.

Dad's purchases at Cash Wise Foods and his excitement about them are legendary in our family. He would charge into the house after his afternoon shift, arriving home around midnight, slamming the door and generally creating noise and mayhem, unconcerned about which baby might be sleeping or what anyone else in the family may be doing.

If I was home and awake when Dad got home, he regaled me with the great deals that he found and carried home in the plastic grocery bags. If he found a particularly great deal, he would call for help carrying in an industrial amount of whatever was in the back of his little Mazda pick-up. If some was good, more was better for Dad. He talked about the future plans for the property, or his great grocery deal finds, but almost never about his work. He hated the factory and the product that they put out. After his years at Kraft dumping toxic chemicals into vats, neither Dad nor I would eat processed cheese.

It must have been for that Y2K tour to Texas that Dad quit his job at Kraft Foods and began traveling full time with the Band. We were beginning to make some real money, with 250 dates per year, and a gross of roughly $500 per show. In fact, Mom started writing each of us kids a check for $253.96 every month, in order to keep her tax burden low. When, at the insistence of her accountant, she announced this new plan, I felt that this would be a huge windfall for my previously non-existent personal finances; I would have some spending money!

In my mind, if I had a paycheck, I was getting closer to being able to support a family. I realized over time, however, that she was expecting us to pay for our personal needs with that money. Personal responsibility with my finances was completely foreign to me, and I blamed her for my struggles. She would chip in for a major medical event, but by and large our money went quickly each month for books, socks, underwear, etc. It took a great deal of discipline to save any, and we had no practice with managing money, so none of us were doing much saving.

Dad finally had his dream kingdom. His every thought was on how he could expand it, and we kids were soldiers and laborers in that conquest. As Grandpa Carpenter's new wife and our addicted Uncle Rick drew Grandpa's bank accounts down, I felt Dad looking to us kids for finances. And our music dream gave him access to everything we made - through Mom. If I complained about the way my money was spent, I would endure hours of railing (from Mom) about how I did not understand what it took, and how I had a problem with greed and money. I learned not to mention my concerns.

Instead I, like everyone in our family, would get as many jobs as I could handle around my home-schooling.

We "pushed turkeys" in the middle of the night, helping to herd them and get them loaded on to big trucks for slaughter. It is, to this day, the worst job I have ever worked in my life. Terribly stinky, and always at night. It paid $9/hour though, so we all did it together anytime a local barn was "loading out;" it was an incredibly high wage for farm kids to get. We walked beans and picked rocks out of farm fields during the day. My sisters started a vastly successful cleaning business, ending up with 30 homes and businesses that they cleaned every week. The rest of us would help them on weekends whenever we had a lot of shows. My buddy, Sarah's bass-playing boyfriend, and I started a lawn and landscaping business. All receipts went to Mom, and were managed by her.

The money would be divvied up between construction projects on the farm, the music business, and personal needs like dentists, clothing, etc. I don't think that any of us kids learned how to manage money at all. We went through Mom for everything. Later, I would realize that we pumped untold thousands of dollars into the farm, an asset that stayed firmly in my parents' hands. We mortgaged it several times to afford the next big thing for the band, three adoptions, and many, many construction projects. My dad loves to build; the house is 9,000 square feet. "It's big; not like a mansion, like an anthill," I used to tell friends. In my memory, it had 10 bedrooms, a large library, 2 full kitchens, 2 dining areas, 7 points of entry, 5 bathrooms, 5 common areas and countless closets and miscellaneous areas.

There was a big barn that we built new, a Guest House that we remodeled, a garage that was full of junk, a Granary that was full of junk, the Studio (which wasn't finished until after I left) and several sheds and small out buildings - all full of junk.

It is difficult to justify to myself how many long, hard hours we all worked on that property. 99% of all construction on that mansion and outbuildings was performed by us..... Mom, Dad, and we four older kids. I learned all of the trades from concrete to shingles and everything in between. Those skills have served me well, along with a great work ethic. I did not realize the value of those things at the time.

Dad was adopted, and from that point in his life he was taught to expect to be gifted whatever he needed; he was willing to work hard, but his kingdom-building seemed to always include using someone else's time and energy and resources.

Chapter 6

Caught in the Act

It was 1989, and I was 15. It was the year of sequels, with *Ghostbusters 2, Lethal Weapon 2, and Back to the Future Part 2*. *The Little Mermaid* and *Driving Miss Daisy* debuted in the US, while in China the protests in Tiananmen Square unfolded, and in Germany the fall of the Berlin Wall would result from massive protests on both sides of the wall; the East German Government would also fall in 1989. Pornography was available to more and more people via VCRs and satellite TV, and even the internet. It was feeling like the modern age - except on Eden Road.

I was often holed up in my bedroom, doing my home-school, or reading a steamy, sexually descriptive romance novel. I had always been a voracious reader, and though I still had no idea what most of the sex bits really meant, I had found books in my dad's massive book collection, hoarded rather non-discriminately, that caused my body to react big time. I didn't know why, but verbal descriptions of breasts and heavy breathing and intense seduction worked very well for me as I unknowingly simulated sex for myself, pulling on myself, as Robin Williams said, "…..harder than a John Deere tractor at an Iowa Tractor Pull!"

I knew that I should tell Dad and Mom that there were some dirty books in the Library, but I loved the breast descriptions too much to rat myself out. Whenever we watched TV, which was rare, I was trained (since age 5) to avert my eyes if a scantily clad girl appeared on the screen. Similarly, if I was in public, and a girl had her cleavage on display, I was to look the other way.

I was very obedient on that one, because my mom would catch me looking and I would get in big trouble. It was years before I could look at a woman and not feel weird if she showed some skin. My experience of my own sexuality was pretty odd, and it was not about to improve.

On one particular evening, my bedroom door was uncharacteristically part way open. I was confident that I had some awareness regarding where everyone in the house was, and I had not intended to touch myself as I read, but I was not prepared for the seduction of whatever I was reading. It was really, really hot.

It may have been the one about the tough, lone-wolf cowboy who was being seduced by the wealthy ranch heiress. She found his camp in the middle of the night, and of course he heard her approach. She was well aware of his attention across the campfire as she removed her jacket. And then her blouse. He sucked in his breath when she removed her bra. She ran her hands over her belly and then ...lower.

It may have been the one about the nearly-naked Russian call girl/spy who pushed the dashing British spy into his own bed and straddled him while she undid his zipper. Her hands and curves carefully hid the weapon in the waistband of her maid's outfit. In the ensuing heat of passion, his hands slid smoothly around her. The two locked in a kiss at the exact moment that both their hands closed on the pistol grip. In the tense struggle for domination of the weapon, their bodies brushed roughly against each other; he rolled on top of her, and they both gasped as the gun fell to the floor, forgotten, as their bodies were joined in passion.

Whichever book it was that night, I did not remain in a mental state to notice much of what was going on in the house around me.

My body was responding in a raging fashion. I read and re-read the juiciest bits, while my hands found myself under the sheets. I pulled the sheets back for easier access. As the characters in the book had their climax, I exploded.

As my body convulsed, my mother walked into my room to say good night.

I felt the most ridiculous mixture of feelings; shame, ecstasy, fear, release, and confusion. My mind could not manage it, and I had no conscious thought.

Mom registered shock and asked, "WHAT are you DOING?" as I scrambled to cover the squirting evidence of my passion. Still no words or thoughts.

At first, my mother was kind. She did not hit me, or throw me out of her house, neither of which would have surprised me. She sat down weakly in the chair by my door, and had a conversation with me.

She lowered the boom gently.

She informed me that this was very wrong. I already knew that she thought men were sexual pigs, so I was aware that I was completing that picture for her and felt deep remorse.

"I'm really sorry, Mom." I mumbled, scarlet-faced, finally able to think again.

She offered to help me control this sinful urge. She said that I should tell her every time that I did this in the future, and that, as a punishment for my self-pleasuring, I would need to fast (go a full 24-hour period with nothing but water).

She was going to help me stay accountable. She also promised that Dad would be having "the talk" with me soon.

He did. It was decidedly unhelpful, and awkward. He clearly had been told to talk to me, and his heart was not in it. After a perfunctory description of what I was currently experiencing, and making sure that I understood that there were any number of immoral and awful sexual proclivities out there, he launched into descriptions of gay sex. I had not yet considered the possibility of gay sex, and his description of men licking certain parts of each other totally freaked me out.

By the time Dad was done speaking, I had exactly zero questions that I was willing to ask. It was all wrong, that was clear. All sex was bad and wrong. Dad's "Talk" did absolutely nothing good for me.

I didn't follow Mom's prescription for "purity," though I tried to. For the next 12 years I tried. I would go 3-6 months being "good." During those times, I would get so horny that if a woman bent over in front of me she was unknowingly in mortal danger of pregnancy. It could have been laughable, if it wasn't so miserable. When I read about men in other cultures who were trying so hard to be pure and chaste, I deeply understood why they might choose to blow themselves up or why they may be angrily waving machine guns or beheading their enemies. I was a very frustrated man. And then I would fall off the wagon. Hardcore. "My way," continued to be reading romance novels, because they were the only access that I had to any kind of descriptions of sex. It really worked for me.

After the climax, or five, would come the guilt and shame. Sometimes I would do the "right" thing, according to Mom, and I would tell her that I had done it, and she would ask how many times, and I would lie.

"Once."

It was bullshit.

But I knew Mom. If I told her the truth - 27 times in one week for instance - I would literally be fasting for that many days. I was sure that in our holy, Gospel-preaching family I was the only routine sinner. I liked this sex stuff. And I would constantly fantasize about actually having a girlfriend. But until age 27, I was too afraid of the consequences from my mom and dad to try that. I was a virgin; in fact, I had not so much as kissed a girl until age 27. It became clear to me; if I wanted to keep doing the music that I loved in the family Band, I would not be dating.

Mom and Dad were not getting along. Some of the fights and hurts that had started early on in their marriage had devolved into bitterness, resentment, and finally cold avoidance. That coldness would be broken abruptly with fights that would last all night; comprised mostly of her yelling and goading him into a response, and him literally falling asleep in his chair whenever she took a breath. So she hardly ever took a breath. And he hardly ever tried to defend himself in any way. I have never seen a person as passive-aggressive as my dad; he never fought, but he never lost either. It drove her crazy. She began enrolling us into their fights, using family discussions that were like Gripe Night, becoming better and more skillful at mob control and at abusing her political enemies in the family with managed "democracy."

When it came to fixing or maintaining anything, my dad only did what he wanted to. The farm's well had to be managed carefully in droughts, because we consistently ran out of water. The upstairs toilet, that we kids used, would not flush properly. One of the girls had a nightmare about firemen responding to our house being on fire and in the dream she was asking them to flush the toilet for us - since they had the big hose. If I took a rather large poo upstairs, it could become quite an embarrassing altercation. These simple maintenance issues seemed to be entirely too much for Dad, though he could design the most ingenious additions to the house. The first such addition was three stories tall, but built on a four-inch-thick slab with no footing; it was not to code, and was guaranteed to shift and crack under the weight ...which it proceeded to do almost immediately. The front staircase, by contrast, spiralled up three floors, was hand-built, and mathematically perfect.

When Mom had enough nagging Dad about the many outstanding maintenance items, she began to get bitter. She began to say, "Fine, me and Joshua will fix it." I became Dad's replacement. The payoff for me was my mother's love, and I was not fully aware that I was trading my father's respect for it, and my own autonomy. I assumed that he was just glad that he didn't have to do the things that she was asking of him.

I took great pride in taking care of Mom, and keeping our family together and loving each other. And she seemed to rely more and more heavily on me as the man of the house - and the only man in the Band, out on the road. I drove the bus, fixed things, set up, hauled things, and answered to Mom in every matter.

At home, I did projects at her direction and only helped Dad if Mom gave me permission. Dad had very little say in anything politically, but his passive aggressive abilities still kept him getting whatever he wanted in his own way. He was absolutely masterful at convincing Mom to spend money. I often felt like a shrewd diplomat, trying to manage two different equal and powerful entities.

I wanted to date a girl; but it was very clear now that I would need to choose between The Carpenter Family Singers and a love life. I learned the fullness of this through the most painful night of my life, emotionally. I have defined abuse for myself as forcing someone to do something that they do not want to do. Because sometimes, abuse is not physical, and sometimes it leaves no marks.

This night happened in late fall of 1994. In the U.S., President Bill Clinton took office, and the Dallas Cowboys beat the Buffalo Bills in the Super Bowl. Tonya Harding pleaded guilty to obstructing justice as she attempted to cover up her involvement in the attack on her figure-skating competitor, Nancy Kerrigan. Rocker Kurt Cobain was found dead in his Lake Washington home, apparently commiting suicide a full three days before he was found. In June, we all watched, along with most Americans, a slow-moving white Bronco on TV, and Nicole Brown Simpson and Ron Brown were found murdered outside the home of OJ Simpson. On Eden Road, we had started watching a little bit of TV, and we knew and followed many of these stories. It was interesting to see how my mom got sucked into the OJ Simpson trial. She was sure that he did it.

Kelly Gunter and I met at a concert in Marshall, Minnesota. Sparks flew immediately, and as often is the case, she chased me until I caught her. It didn't take me long to get her invited to one of our big Carpenter Family shindigs.

I was 20, Kelly was 17. Each of us Carpenter kids had become increasingly vocal about our interest in the opposite sex. My sister Leah had a couple of guys that had chased and briefly dated her. Sarah had dated a young man that had been in a landscaping business with me, and had played bass with the Band. A variety of young, eligible friends were coming over to our place where Mom could keep an eye on everything. We would play Dutch blitz, a card game we had learned from our Belizean Mennonite friends. I had wanted to date Anna, one of the kids we met from Belize, but when her dad asked me how I would like living in Belize, I realized that I would not, and let it drop. I had not felt that my mother approved, either, though she claimed that she loved Anna and her family.

On Eden Road, on that very chilly October night, Kelly came over to play cards and games, and get to know me. I loved our parties! We would stay up until the wee hours of the morning, drinking soda and eating chips. We got loud, laughed, and competed mercilessly. Mom was at her best, because she loved parties, games, and movies. She was like one of us kids. I found out later, from my sisters, that none of their friends wanted to date me as a teen, because they felt that Mom was too involved, and dominated me completely. They were right on.

At some point that evening, I took an opportunity to ask Kelly if she wanted to go for a walk. She and I had been winning the couples Blitz tournament. We were so connected, and doing our best to impress each other. This made us a powerful team, and inexplicably infuriated my mom. Mom was very competitive, and I could tell that we should quit playing cards now, as she would just get more and more angry. Besides, I wanted some time to be alone with Kelly. Kelly agreed, and we bundled up for the two mile walk around "the Circle," our standard two-mile hike on the gravel farm roads around our house.

While the girls and their friends chose another game, and Mom put the Little Kids to bed, Kelly and I set out. She was so patient, and really let me do all of the talking. I talked to her like I talked to Kenny. Very theoretical, very philosophical. And in all of that, I fell in love with her. She was fearless, grounded, and fun. She listened, and she wanted to be with me.

I don't know for the life of me why she did. I had to be the strangest experience for her. I did not so much as take her hand, or briefly kiss her. I was very proper. When she went over to the Guest House to join the pajama party with all of the girls, I returned to the Big House to sleep, and I was walking on air.

That air collapsed the minute I got inside the house. I could feel the tension. Mom was pissed. I could always tell. She was polite and cordial at first. How did it go. Good. I'm glad you enjoyed your walk. She is awesome, huh? You really think so?

And then her face darkened, and she got real.

"You will not be seeing her again."

I swallowed hard; my heart sank.

"But I told Kelly that we would write letters, and that I would like to date her," I stammered. Was I really 20 years old?

"Well, you can write her a letter. And you have to end it. She is not like you. Joshua, she is VERY worldly. Did you see her make-up? And her clothes? She is much more into looks and impressing people with her body than your sisters are. This will never work."

I tried for an hour to change her mind, but it was quite made up. She told me that she would want to see the letter that I sent Kelly tomorrow, breaking up with her. Mom said she would help me get it right.

I trudged up the stairs to sleep. With all of the guests in the house, my blankets were on the floor in the Library so one of them could have my bed.

I lay there, with a pain that I had never felt before. It had nothing to do with the hard floor. That pain scarcely registered beneath this other pain. It was not really in my stomach, nor was it exactly where my heart was. I wondered what a heart attack felt like. I did not sleep at all that night.

It was the most intense emotional pain; I could not believe or verbalize, as I writhed on the blankets, trying to make it go away, how badly I hurt. I felt entirely powerless, and I felt a sense of loss, and grief, and anger, and shame.

The beautiful love that I had felt a mere hour earlier felt like something horrible and awful now. I somehow understood that if I was really committed to Kelly, I would have stood up to Mom. If it was for real, I would not let that love die so easily. In fact, that was part of the pain; I hated myself intensely for not having the balls to stand up for this girl that I thought I loved. For not having the courage to stand up for what my heart wanted. To stand up for me. It was a brutal wake up call.

But I could not have put any of that into words that night.

I knew that I would do exactly as Mom had said. And even though Dad liked Kelly, he would never get involved in this, I knew. It was over.

In the morning, I did what Mom said, and for the first time (but not the last) she helped her 20-something son draft a proper break-up letter.

During my twenties, as I remained celibate and frustratedly tried to abstain in every way, I would fall off of the wagon. When I did, I would push the boundaries of my environment, trying to find a sexual outlet. We were traveling and working a LOT.

Most days were either driving in the bus all day to go sing somewhere, or long practice sessions, or regular maintenance on clothing, equipment, etc. Even though we saw most of the U.S., we were workaholics, and almost never stopped to see the sites.

When we were at home in Minnesota, we worked on the property. We worked on building projects too numerous to name here. We were very late to adopt computers, or the internet, and even when we did, it was for the express purpose of the music business. Only Mom had any real access, and porn was completely unknown to me at that time. I was aware that there were magazines out there like Playboy and Hustler, but I would not dare even look at them for fear that Mom would find out and punish me. Worse, God knew at all times what I was doing and what I was looking at, and my view of Him was an extension of my parents, so I had no doubt that my punishment would be swift and harsh should I stray into "bad magazines."

I found other sexual outlets, however.

At home, I had access to my family's massive book collection and those racy romance novels that would feed my need for some understanding of sex. It was all I could get. I knew that I was "wrong" to be reading them, but I could not stop myself.

Before I left home, and had a girlfriend who explained how sex worked to me, I was very curious. We lived on a farm; I had watched animals "mating," but I struggled to understand the connection between what they were doing and what my body was craving so deeply. Masturbation felt like a very cheap substitute for what I really wanted. On two different occasions, I used my fingers to explore and stimulate female animals on our farm. They did not like it, and my body did not respond, so it ended, because it didn't do anything for me other than raise more questions. But I did it; I tried it; and I knew it was wrong. I still feel intense shame over my actions; it just sounds so weird and sad to me now.

I did not restrain or force the animals in any way; I was just really, painfully curious.

Chapter 7   Cindy
September 11, 2001

     The Carpenter Family Singers spent the entire day of September 11th, 2001, in our living room in Morgan, Minnesota, watching and rewatching the awful destruction, and trying to somehow grasp the meaning of all of this death and hate and seemingly needless pain. I was 27, and the endless cycle of hate and retribution in the world had lurched forward onto the next predictable cog; millions of Americans were already festering a painful and toxic seed of bitterness and hate towards any target that seemed appropriate. Who did this to us? Who will be next? What can we do to protect ourselves? The news channels seemed to suggest that it was militant Islam, and that the individual targets of our anger, presumably terrorists, were very difficult to pinpoint. It seemed that Islam, much like Christianity, had very noble beliefs, but also had a militant few that used their religion to justify hate and murder. Our little family band suddenly seemed small and inconsequential that day. I felt helpless, paralyzed, and off-balance.

     As the music group had developed, we had attracted friends, helpers, and romantic interests. Cindy was all of the above. Cindy was 5'2" tall, with piercing blue eyes and long blonde hair. She was curvy in all the right places, but had a walk that was decidedly masculine and a manner that was a bit rough. She had a hardness to her face and eyes that reverberated pain and heartache. I loved her for being fearless.

As the bombing of the Twin Towers played over and over, she was in our living room, on the phone with her mom, Karen. They talked for a long time, and 18-year-old Cindy was apparently considering returning immediately to be with her mother in case of a deepening national crisis. Things were so uncertain at that moment; we all felt that even invasion could be imminent. We were stunned and glued to the news coverage. We all felt the urge, like Cindy, to reach out to those who were important to us. We had absolutely no idea what to expect next, or how to respond.

In the end, Karen and Cindy decided that the 6-hour trip back to Rapid City, South Dakota could be made easily if some further threat required it, but that for now, Cindy would stay and finish helping out the Carpenter Family Singers. Mom was already on the phone with our video production people creating a commemorative patriotic video to be offered at our upcoming Video Release Party in December. In addition to our first-ever Carpenter Family Singers Music Video, this other project would really be something special; a worship song imposed over video of eagles and flags and the burning buildings that would show our support for America, and also bring a little extra income to the Band. Gradually, the deafening feeling receded from our souls, and we began to return to life again.

So Cindy was staying, and I was thrilled.

Cindy

I had wanted to date for some time. I was 27 years old, and 6'5" tall. I was athletic, good looking, and very intelligent. I had an intuitive understanding of people's feelings. I was desperately horny; but I had not, as yet, dated a girl. Some of our fans may have wondered privately if I was the quietly gay or sexually uncertain piano player who would always stay by his mother's side. I could have been. But I was massively unhappy.

I had not always felt this strong attraction to girls; when I was 13, I was vastly opposed to them. My mom's friend Terry Seaborg asked me what I had against girls, after some derisive comment that I had made. I grasped at a straw. "Their eye shadow!" I blurted. "Looks like their eyes are MOLDING!" We all had a good laugh. And Terry said something that I was to remember often, later, "Well that is GOING to change soon!" she said with a laugh and an eye-roll. Somehow I sensed that she was telling the truth, and I wondered what she knew that I did not.

We met Cindy and her mother, Karen, in Rapid City, South Dakota. They had moved there in order for Karen to escape a murderous ex-husband, and as a result of severe trauma from that first relationship, they stayed hidden in society, with a very small circle of friends. Cindy was the youngest of four, though the others were all out of the home by the time that I met them. Cindy was home-schooled, similar to us Carpenter kids. But unlike us, she had not been very disciplined (nor had her mother), so she was not actually doing much schooling. She and her mother were extremely close, and they trusted almost no one outside of each other. But they trusted us for some reason.

Karen and Cindy would show up to our concerts in the Rapid City area, and share some time and conversation with us. When we first met them, Cindy was 16 and wore dresses all of the time. This would change as she slowly broke away from her mother's influence, but I noticed her dresses with a very appreciative eye, because I thought they looked very respectful and ladylike.

Cindy became close with my sisters. They were like mentors to her, and Karen was very glad for their influence, because Cindy was wanting friends and was being very negatively steered by her wild siblings and her even wilder friends back in Rapid City. My sisters looked like what Karen envisioned for Cindy; respectful, obedient, Christian young women.

Arguably the kindest of the older sisters in my family was Sarah, the middle of the three; she spent more time with Cindy than anyone else, and Cindy adored her. As we returned every year to Rapid City, we saw Cindy mature and change. She started wearing jeans and boots, or big baggy sweats. She went from looking very shy and innocent to having a hard and pained look on her face at times.

Earlier that summer of 2001, as we plowed headlong into endless work on the show at the Hart Ranch Arena, we were completely oblivious to most of the news, and were allowed to watch none of the current movies out in theaters. The Bush Tax Cuts were signed into law by President George "W" Bush, a 60-car train derailment occurred in a tunnel in Baltimore, Maryland, *Jurassic Park III* premiered, and Lance Armstrong was disqualified from the Tour De France for doping. The Colorado Avalanche won their second-ever Stanley Cup, and Cindy began coming out to the show often, falling in love with the lights, the music, and the family.

She became a regular visitor, willing to help with anything in order to hang out and be a part of things. The sound and light crew and the maintenance crew loved her and appreciated her willingness to assist. She worked with me often, as I was in charge of set-up and take-down, and she didn't need special skills to help with that. My sisters were becoming too busy and "sissified" to pitch in on the heavy lifting like they used to, so Cindy and I settled into a very platonic, almost guy-friend back-and-forth kind of relationship, hauling and setting up gear.

After a hectic and successful season in the Arena, and as we prepared to close up the show and go back to Minnesota and the Farm in Morgan, Mom invited Cindy to go with us for a couple of months, and help out with a very busy concert and building schedule back in Minnesota. Cindy and Karen accepted happily. Every Spring and Fall, when we returned home from a tour, Dad had a very aggressive list of projects for us to complete, keeping us busy for most of a 12 hour day, 6-7 days a week. We older kids had begun to dread the never-ending projects and back-breaking work that it took to do it Dad's way.

Dad's way was always the very hard, cheap way, and involved lots of labor on our part. One summer, years earlier, my sister Sarah had nightmares about mowing the five-acre lawn at the farm with scissors, because Dad had (in real life) been "too busy" to fix the riding lawn mower. I had been mowing all five acres with a push mower - I mowed the farm with that push mower all summer.

As she helped out at the farm, Cindy worked with me a lot. By summer's end, a couple of my sisters didn't get along with her very well anymore, and Sarah was becoming uneasy about her own relationship with Cindy for a completely different reason. I loved Cindy's help, however, and we became better friends than ever.

At the end of her two month stay, Cindy followed the Band to help out at a very big show that we did every year in Rochester, Minnesota, for the Midwest Gospel Quartet Association.

On the way to Rochester, Cindy drove a pale yellow Lincoln Continental that my mom had decided to give her. Cindy did not own a car when she came out to the farm, and had originally planned to take a Greyhound bus back home. Since Cindy had not been paid a wage for any of her work, besides room and board, Mom decided to give her the car as a token of appreciation. The plan was for Cindy to drive that car home to Rapid City and go back to her job at Papa John's Pizza, and hopefully reset her life to something more positive than it had been when she left with us.

As the Quartet Convention in Rochester wrapped up, I became aware of a heartache that had been growing. I did not want to say good-bye to Cindy.

The two of us were hauling the last of the stuff out to the bus from the Convention Center, when I stopped her.

"Cindy!"

"Yeeeesss...." She turned slowly on one heel.

I was suddenly breathless for no good reason and very nervous.

"Thank you!" was all I was able to stammer.

"Okkkkayyy....." a bemused smile played around her lips.

"You are welcome ...?" she said, eyebrows arching inquisitively.

"No. really!" I realized that I seriously wanted to thank her. I awkwardly thrust out my hand. How does one talk to girls like this?

I smiled, "I really appreciate your hard work. You have helped me out immensely."

Cindy's ice-blue eyes sparkled, while she shook my hand, and still looking a bit unsure of what I was after, said a bit more convincingly, "Well, I really enjoyed doing it. You are great to work with."

That lump in my throat! Why did she have to be so damned pleasant and professional!

"I am going to really miss you...." my tone was suddenly very sober, and she felt it.

She looked me straight in the eyes and said, very sincerely this time, "I am going to miss you, too."

I gulped and took the plunge.

"I thought that maybe we could write letters...." I said, almost offhandedly, with a little fake bravado.

Cindy looked a little surprised. But she answered firmly and without hesitation, "Yes, that would be nice."

I beamed from ear to ear. "Cool!"

In my relief and excitement, I roughed up her curly, blonde hair and we raced each other to the door back into the Convention Center. I was flying higher than I ever had before.

I was going to date Cindy!

The Carpenter Family Singers hit the road that night, as planned, for points east and south. We had quite an aggressive itinerary: Iowa, Ohio, New York, Virginia, and finally Florida - where we were planning to embark on our first holiday as a music group.

An entire week on a cruise, the whole family; no work, no singing, just relaxing. It was one of Mom's dreams for us; our Biblical version of partying down. By this time, The Carpenter Family Singers were extremely successful in Texas, Arizona, South Dakota, Minnesota, and even into California; going East would be a new challenge, and fill up our schedule even tighter.

As our big blue-and-white tour bus, with the nine submarine-style bunks and "The Carpenter Family Singers" emblazoned across both sides cruised its way south and east out of Minnesota that night, Cindy steered the pale, yellow Lincoln west, back to South Dakota.

We were in Ohio before I worked up the courage to tell my family that I had committed to writing letters to Cindy. Letter writing was a very serious thing for our family, and none of them would miss the romantic implications. Christian courtship was to allow for no opportunities for "impropriety," and letter writing was the gold standard for getting to know your date without being tempted to touch or kiss.

Even though I was doing it "right," I was blindsided by the strong reaction - the family was furious. What ensued was 6 hours or more long, in a hotel room graciously provided for us by our Mennonite friends in Sugarcreek, Ohio. Six-hour fights were not unusual for Mom; but this one I had not expected.

We had a concert the next day, but we stayed up very late, into the small hours of the morning, as they informed me that I would, in fact, NOT be writing romantic letters to Cindy.

They told me how Cindy had told Sarah in confidence that she had had an abortion, and how she thought that she might be gay. Cindy had, they said, insinuated that she was romantically interested in Sarah. I was made to understand that she was not - in any way - a good fit for me.

They gave me every reason why this was a very stupid idea of mine, and, in the end, wore me down with brute emotional strength. I did not agree with them; I cried, and pleaded, and got angry, and tried to be stubborn. But after six hours, they had won, and I woodenly let my mother help me craft a "Dear John" letter to Cindy. It was very similar to the letter to Kelly Gunter that Mom had written for me seven years earlier. This letter would politely and firmly end the relationship, and would sever all ties between me and Cindy.

Less than two hours after falling into bed crushed and exhausted, my alarm went off and we were all getting on the bus to go to the Mennonite church and preach the power of family. When the alarm jangled, I woke up to a new feeling in my heart.

I was so angry, deep down. I was not typically an angry person. What began in that hotel room, and in the weeks following, resulted in a silent fury in me. I was no longer the same person I used to be. I became cynical, and consciously mistrusted my mother. A pain that had started some years earlier with my first attempted date had blossomed into complete frustration and a feeling of no longer being on the same team.

My mother did not care about me finding a girlfriend, I now realized. No one would pass her standards. It would just be no; the answer would always be no. She did not care that I was extremely sexually frustrated. She didn't think that I SHOULD be sexually frustrated. My sisters could date, and have her blessing. I never would get that, and I would never be allowed to make mistakes and learn it for myself.

Mom made sure that I sent the break-up letter the next day, making a special stop at a mail drop to ensure that it went out.

I did not hear anything from Cindy while we toured the Southeast, and I assumed that she had written me off. I was wrong.

It would not be the end of Cindy in my life, and it would not be the last time that my mother and I would argue over this issue. But for that tour, I was a compliant, 27-year-old piano player, traveling with the Carpenter Family Singers, enjoying the journey and the perks of being in a nationally touring Band.

Chapter 8
The Turning Point

One month later, Cindy surprised us all and drove that same pale, yellow Lincoln Continental to our first show back home, which was held in Sioux Falls, South Dakota. Cindy was truly fearless. When I saw her in the parking lot, I was very surprised, and instantly attracted again.

I had kept to the family rule; there had been no contact with Cindy after Ohio. But here in Sioux Falls, seeing her again, I knew in my heart that I would no longer stick to the rule. Since Ohio, I felt no more allegiance to my mother, nor would I be sharing my heart with her any longer. What had started with lying about masturbating had matured into complete distrust. She had gone from being my ally to being the enemy - but I did not let her see this change.

The interactions that day at the concert in Sioux Falls were beyond awkward. I was feeling guilty for standing Cindy up with no real explanation - and deeply attracted to her. I was being studiously careful to hide my feelings from my mother - in fact, from everyone, as my sisters would certainly report me to my mother. Cindy was aloof and cold to me, and she seemed overjoyed to see the little siblings and the girls. Mom was very crisp and business like, with her standard, fake, tone that told anyone that knew her that she was not pleased to be forced into dealing with this person.

Sarah seemed extremely stressed. Of course, Cindy's presence refreshed in my mind the stories I had been told about her being a lesbian and I found myself watching her and Sarah to see if there was anything there. The only thing that I saw was that Sarah seemed very tense.

We did the show, and Cindy helped set up and tear down, and helped the little ones get dressed for the show, just like she always had. I wanted to talk things out with Cindy, with no way to do so without being discovered by Mom. Before I could fathom what was happening, or find a way to chat privately with Cindy, my mother was inviting her to come to the farm again and help for the month of December, before we left for the Texas/Arizona tour.

I was in complete and utter disbelief at this decision of my mother's. Why invite Cindy, who had clearly been a huge distraction for Sarah and I, and caused so much family drama, back to the farm? I had no answer. Mine was not the only drama that Mom dealt with in any given day, and she clearly did not understand where my heart was; she seemed to believe that she had succeeded in controlling my romantic interest. Also, I was learning that my mom and my dad really only seemed to value people who could help them build up the farm. It seemed that free labor was a very motivating factor for them. I just could not understand this decision to bring Cindy back to Eden Road.

During the next week my life would change forever.

On a bright, windy, December day in southern Minnesota, with golden leaves swirling around the yard, and a crisp chill in the air, huge tractors pulling bright red and rusty yellow wagons full of harvested corn were roaring up and down the farm roads around our house. Off in the distance, across the gently rolling hills, billowing dust clouds showed where today's frantic, last-minute harvesting was happening. On the news, Enron was filing for Bankruptcy, *Oceans 11* was premiering, and Peter Jackson's "*The Fellowship of the Ring*" was finally coming to theaters.

We were paying attention to none of it. Other than watching the Minnesota Vikings play football, and an occasional exhausted break for a movie on the VCR, we were all working very hard getting ready for our first-ever Video Release Party. More intense than usual, we were working at least 12 hours every day, seven days a week. I was the stage manager, and handled all the technical aspects of the concert, and Cindy was helping me. We had, as we worked together, developed a slightly aloof and professional tone towards each other. At one point, we were getting things from the Guest House; it was just the two of us.

In the relative privacy, I was sweating, and there was a knot in my stomach. Now was my chance. We had hardly touched more than awkward hugs (each member of my family ALWAYS gave you a hug when they first arrived or saw you, and another when you left).

I stopped and turned to face Cindy. She could feel the energy shift and grounded herself.

"Yes?" she asked, a trifle coldly, as she searched my eyes.

"Would you still like to write letters?" I asked weakly.

She considered carefully. Her eyes softened, as she noticed the tears starting to form in my eyes. And then she hardened again.

"You should know that a lot of girls would not have been very nice about what you did."

I looked down. "I know."

I offered no explanation. How does one begin to explain that my mom wrote it for me? I was just beginning to understand how odd our family culture might seem to the rest of the world. I didn't know what to say.

She rescued me.

"I was really tore up. A lot of girls would have tried to hurt you back. Like get somebody to fuck up your shit." It was like cold water in the face, both the thinly veiled threat, and the words that we had never been allowed to use. At the age of 27, I was not entirely sure exactly what that meant. What precisely would happen to me if someone was to "Fuck up my shit?" I was in way over my head.

What I had done was wrong, and I knew that for sure. I looked up. "I'm really sorry."

She softened again. I knew I needed to warn her before she agreed to anything further.

"My mom won't like it at all." I looked directly at her. That was a massive understatement.

I watched Cindy's eyes for her response, and I loved her for it.

"I don't think it's any of her business." Her eyes flashed, and then steeled, "I really don't care, Josh."

I loved her in that moment because together, we stood up to my mother.

My personal test was just minutes away; it would be my turning point.

We left the Guest House without so much as touching. We had simply agreed to write letters, and explore the possibilities; we were both clear that there would be a price to pay.

I told Mom about it a few minutes later, over in the Big House. I was resolved, and I had given my word to Cindy. I was standing in the addition to the house, looking through what used to be an exterior window, and had been remodeled into what we called a "Pass-through"- a neatly trimmed, 4-foot-wide opening from the old kitchen out into the entry way by the front door. I was scared to death. I had never fully defied my mother, in all of my 27 years. Not openly and honestly, anyway.

"Mom," I said. She turned, as if in slow motion, and you could see in her eyes that she could feel that something was about to happen. "I talked to Cindy."

Her eyes were focusing. Burning holes in my face as she realized what was coming.

"We are going to write letters," I said. My dry mouth almost stopped the words.

She did not hesitate. I play it over and over in my mind. She did not hesitate.

"Then you're out." It was final.

We stared at each other for a moment. This was where I had always caved in before. This was where, even as a 27-year-old man, I would usually start crying. I could not go to the level that she was prepared to go to.

But this time I did. I looked her dead in the eyes and said, "Okay."

Now I saw shock and hesitation; and stony resolve again. She turned back to whatever she was doing. I was shaking.

It was my turning point. I was risking everything that I knew and loved for something that I didn't even know (for sure) existed. I had spent 12 years building the Carpenter Family Singers, and developing the property that I called home; 27 years in a very isolated, insulated, family unit that was my everything.

I was bringing my kingdom crashing down around my ears for what? I would no longer be "one of us;" and why? For freedom; to be allowed to make my own mistakes. To take the chance that what was out there was better than Mom and Dad said it was. That I was better than they said I was.

"You will never make it in the real world," Mom and Dad had both said over and over, "You don't know what it's like out there!"

I was going to find out, and Cindy would help me. We would get married, and have babies, and I would have sex for the first time. I tried to imagine kissing a girl; kissing Cindy. We were already in love - I was not going back on this decision. I was clear on that; I would be sorely tested.

Escaping the Cult

I wondered if Dad would back Mom's decree.

The next two days were beyond awkward. I was completely integral to all of the technical aspects of our video release party, so I was constantly interfacing with the family, but I was already being shunned emotionally. My Grandma Dori came 300 miles down to the Farm from International Falls to celebrate with us. Grandma, whom I loved to pieces, had always loved me deeply. She also loves my mom deeply. And she was fairly unaware of the abuses that happened when she was not visiting. Later, I think that Grandma had some suspicions, but she apparently did not want to confront my mother. I don't know why.

Though she must have noticed the tension, Grandma Dori didn't say anything to me about it; I am sure that Mom and Dad filled her in on my "rebellion."

We had many, many logistical issues to deal with, setting up for the concert of our lives. Our big show was being held at the brand new, state-of-the-art, Redwood Falls High School, and many of our local friends and neighbors were coming - as well as fans from around the country.

As we drove a load of props and equipment to the Performing Arts Center at the High School, we drove through Morgan, my hometown for 14 years. There was a sign on the road leading into town, "Morgan, Where City and Country Meet" and right below that, "Home Of The Carpenter Family." No one in Morgan could know what was going on in our celebrity family that day.

In spite of the off-stage drama, we were pros; the concert went extremely well and we sold a bunch of product. We were reaching a place that less than 1% of all homegrown bands ever reach. We had a huge following! Our mailing list had reached over 10,000 addresses; it seemed that we were on the edge of being a household name.

But the normal visiting after the show, and the jubilant celebrations, were very hollow and distant for me, because I knew that it was my last time. Twelve years working to this point; and if Mom stuck to her guns I was done tomorrow. On the way home that night, after tearing down everything, and packing it into the bus for the trip back to the Farm, it was just me and Dad taking the last load, probably around midnight. As we cruised the 30 or so miles from the High School to the Farm, I tried to work up the courage to talk to Dad. I was nervous about his opinion, because while Mom might change her mind, Dad never did. If he was done with me, then I was truly done. I didn't want to leave, but I had to know. We were almost all the way home, a stiff, awkward silence of 25 minutes before I could force the words out.

"Is Mom serious about me leaving tomorrow?" I asked, timidly.

Dad turned in the bus-driver's seat, with that stubborn look that he gets when he is annoyed.

"Yeah, I guess so," he said.

I swallowed hard. I thought so. I had, earlier in the day, told Mom that I would be happy to stay on, in my capacity as piano player and stage manager in order to fill out our bookings for the coming tour year. In answer, she simply repeated that if I was pursuing Cindy, then I was out on Monday. It became clear that she was fully expecting to cave my resolve.

It was Sunday night, and I tried one last desperate time for leniency. I had always seen Dad as the softy, because he didn't yell or hit like Mom did. I learned that he was a different kind of hard.

"Do you agree with this, Dad? I just want to write to Cindy!" I sounded desperate, broken almost.

He turned again and looked me straight in the eyes. "Yes, Joshua, I do."

I looked down, and my cheeks were hot. I felt very still inside, with a pain that I could not describe. And very focused.

That night, I packed up my little bedroom full of stuff. Since all or our money went to the Band, and was disbursed by Mom, I had very few possessions. I did not own a car. I sat there on the edge of my bed that actually belonged to Mom. Everything belonged to Mom. I stared at the floor for a while, somewhat numb, thinking about how I would leave with no car. We owned 6 cars, but they were all in Mom's name.

The next morning, I asked her about it. How could I leave if I had no car? She said she would sell me the Oldsmobile out back. It was a piece of crap, parked on the weeds in the back parking lot of the studio, with the driver's-side mirror hanging by the wiring, and the paint peeling; it hadn't been started in who-knows-how-long. I had no other choices.

"How much?" I asked. Whatever it was, we both knew that I would be paying it.

"$1500." I looked down, feeling screwed over and grateful at the same time.

I had a feeling, even with my very limited car-valuing experience, that she was really getting her money's worth out of me. But at least my car problem was solved.

"Okay," I said.

Mom knew where my money was; she had until recently been signatory to my bank account. I had been allowed to put about $2500 into my savings account when I was working full-time as an electrician last summer; it was supposed to be for me to start learning to save. The check that I would write her for the car would be over half of my savings, and I had no idea whatsoever, at the age of 27, what it would cost to live out on my own.

By the time I had everything packed up, it was late afternoon, and the bank was already closed in Morgan. I hadn't thought that through. I paused at Mom's office.

I went in, and I endured an hour of her ranting, as she did when she was very upset. I thought with a tremor of another time that she had been this upset. It was the time that we adult kids confronted her as a group over something; the time that Gripe Night turned on her. I was more than a little afraid that she would kick and scream and lose it now.

She railed on in a similarly unhinged fashion; she screamed, accused, and brought up all of my past sins. I was deeply embarrassed, as the rest of the Carpenter Family Singers were in the office as well. I did not give in. I handed her a check for the car that was already loaded.

"I will have to transfer it from savings," I said, "then the check will be good."

She snorted. "It better BE......!" the last word uncertain, as if weighing her ultimatum, "I am depositing it first thing in the morning! And if it bounces, the cops will be after you!"

I gulped.

My sister Sarah remembers from that night that soft-hearted Melita at one point joined the attack and sputtered, "I hope you get hit by a car!"

Melita hated conflict, but could be extremely vicious when angry. The other adults admonished her that she was overdoing it.

But no one said a word when Mom took over the attack.

"I think you are filled with an evil SPIRIT!" she shouted. That really shook me, as she knew it would. I had no way of knowing if that might be true. I didn't feel possessed - but I had never acted this way before.

"I am leaving, Mom." I turned to go.

She freaked out again. "WAIT HERE!" she shrieked.

It was awkward standing there with my family members, bandmates, and closest group of friends up until this point in my life; all of them hard-faced and angry. I went back outside into the frigid evening air. Why was I waiting? Because I had been doing what she ordered me to do for 27 years, that is why. I wished I hadn't.

I had been like a parent to the three "Little Kids." Mom was busy running the business, and frankly, I was no longer sure if she even liked parenting them, or parenting at all anymore. She gloried in the music business, and spent most of her energy there. As a result of this, and her increasingly extreme moods, some of us stepped up and parented them. It was safer for them if we helped them. I felt very close to each of them.

Mom came back outside, from the Big House, with all three kids in tow, and all three bawling.

"Tell them!" she shrilled. "Tell them you are just LEAVING them!!"

"Look them in the eyes! Look what you are doing to them!

They all started sobbing with fresh fervor. Their hearts were being ripped out. And in all of this drama, at 8, and 10, and 10, their reactions were very real. I almost caved in; but I did not. It was heart-rending, and I could not think of any way that I could help them. With tears in my eyes, and head hung low, I walked to the old car and got in. I could hardly see well enough to get out of the driveway and onto Eden Road safely. I hurt.

Chapter 9
Escape from the Cult

My mother banished Cindy on the day that I announced our decision to write to each other, and Cindy left immediately. It was the day before the Video Release Party that she had worked so hard to help set up. But she would not get to see it. She packed up her pale yellow Lincoln and drove back to Rapid City. On the Farm I had no cell phone, and the land line was not mine, so for the next couple of days I had no contact with Cindy. She went home to Karen.

Cindy was given a car to leave with, ostensibly because she had not been paid for her work of three months. I had worked for 12 years in the family music business and was forced to spend over half of the money that I had saved from my tiny paychecks to purchase an overpriced car to leave in.

It was many years before I could even admit that it was not the way I wanted to be treated, and that it was not fair and equitable treatment at all. The night that I left however, I wasn't thinking about fair treatment; I was scared to death that the cops were right behind me because my check might have bounced. It didn't, and I had a cell phone, an apartment, and a job as an electrical apprentice within 24 hours of sleeping in my car that first night that I left home. It was an eternal, terrifying night. It was 20 degrees below zero at a truck stop in Sioux Falls, South Dakota, and I started my car several times that night to stay warm as I tried to sleep. What had I done?!!

There was no obvious logic to choosing Sioux Falls, other than that I was running. I believed that everyone in the family and even my best friend would side with Mom, and send me back to the Farm in humiliation if I were to reach out to them.

The next weeks were a whirlwind of amazing new experiences and uncomfortable freedom. Cindy and Karen worried about me for two days, and as soon as I had my cell phone we began burning up the airways. Those two brave women were my much-needed support in those first couple weeks. My Aunt Christie Pullar sent me a box of essentials for my new apartment, and my Grandma Dori came to visit me after a couple of weeks. Their love and support has always been of the utmost value to me. They likely paid a price with my mom for it.

As soon as they knew that I had a place, Cindy and Karen loaded up the Lincoln, rented a U-Haul, and brought all of the furniture that they thought I could use to Sioux Falls. They brought some furniture from Cindy's storage unit and more from Karen's house. They knew that I had only the personal items that I could fit in the back seat of my car. They drove across South Dakota in a blizzard, and nearly froze to death at a gas stop in the middle of the state where they had to wait until 7 am for the gas pumps to be turned on. They made it clear that I was not alone, and that I was loved. We had a great weekend in my new apartment.

On a back road outside of Sioux Falls, SD, after my first official date at a Chinese restaurant, I experienced my first kiss. I thought that it was amazing, and tasted like egg-rolls. I didn't know yet that it could be a lot better. I was about to have my 28th birthday.

Karen and Cindy stayed with me for more than two weeks, over the holidays and until my birthday on January 10. I slept in the nice bed that they brought (I had been sleeping on the floor, with a garbage bag of my clothing as a pillow), and Cindy slept on the couch that they brought. Karen, in her recliner, had to be shut in the walk-in closet in the middle of the night because she tended to sleep-talk, sleep-walk, and keep us up as her very strong sleeping medication kicked in. We all had a good laugh that first morning when she peeked her head out of the closet and said weakly, "Was I bad?"

That first week or two, Cindy and I stayed very proper and only exchanged kisses out on our dates. Karen seemed to appreciate our restraint, and even though she was knocked out every night on her Ambien, we did not even try to mess around.

After the ladies went back to Rapid City, we made heavy use of the cell towers. Everything about this new life was very odd for me, and I would stay up all night sometimes watching programs on TV that I would never have been allowed to watch at home. Jerry Springer was a favorite of mine, before I began to realize that some of the shows were probably staged. I couldn't believe what I was watching. I also noticed the adult book and video store in town, and because I felt extremely anonymous those first few weeks, it occurred to me that no one would ever know if I went in to check out the content. I just didn't feel attracted to it, or maybe I didn't yet dare; I would not visit for years to come.

Cindy had to explain to me over the phone, and eventually show me in person, what part of my anatomy would interface with hers, should we ever decide to have sex. She found it most amusing.

I was determined to do it "right" and not have sex before we were married; that intention would be sorely tested.

I had very little communication with my family; every time we tried to connect, it resulted in them trying to talk me out of my choice, and back to Eden.

The Carpenter Family Singers were in their last year of touring, and experienced a great many changes that I missed, as one sister after another found serious dates and soon married. I would hear later that things at home got crazier after the music group closed for good, and after the "Big Kids," as we oldest four were called, left home.

And most of the craziness centered around my mom.

Chapter 10   Mom

My mom, Jannelle Kay Carpenter, was the second child of Bob and Dori Pullar, of International Falls, Minnesota. She is a 5' 7" tall brunette, with a powerful energy and a love for the spotlight in any room. She makes herself significant in any situation.

When my mom was 2, in 1955, my Grandma Dori was in the hospital with one of her eight pregnancies. Mom and the other kids were being watched by my Great Grandma Ella; Baby Mom was racing around the house and fell into the boiling hot wash water that Grandma Ella was using to clean the laundry. Mom was burned very badly, and not expected to make it through her first night in the hospital. It was an honest accident, but Grandma Ella felt horrible about it for the rest of her life. She and my Aunt June prayed for Mom at the hospital all through the night, and in the middle of the night her fever lifted and she steadily improved. Mom always felt that she had been spared through the power of prayer for something big, and she lived her life with a great sense of purpose and pride.

Dad and Mom met in high school. Dad was very spoiled growing up, according to Mom, because his parents doted on their two adopted charges. Grandpa and Grandma Carpenter were in their fifties when they adopted the boys, and treated the boys more like grandparents might. The boys had every new toy and anything else they may want. Rick, my dad's brother, would take the cash and the freedom and destroy his life with drugs. Mom said that he was an addict, and it was because Grandpa and Grandma Carpenter would not quit giving him money.

Mom did not grow up with money. Her parents worked very hard, but they had eight kids, and my Grandpa drank quite a bit, so the Pullar kids had to get jobs and pay for anything that they wanted with their own earnings.

Mom was very proud of her work ethic, and when she and Dad got married after high school, Dad went to work framing houses with her dad, learning to keep up with Grandpa Pullar's high demands.

Mom had strong opinions about most people and events. She talked all the time about what she thought, and in the privacy of her own home, it only took about 1.2 seconds from the moment the door shut behind someone for her to say what she really thought about them. It was rarely kind.

Dad had very strong opinions as well, but his were about ideas, and world events, and especially his Biblical beliefs. This duo of opinions regarding anyone who entered Eden would be the first thing that we would hear when that person left the farm; Mom, regarding her judgements of them, and Dad, assessing whether they fit our belief system, or if they were too "worldly." It was one of the ways that we all learned to influence each others' opinions of each new person we met; and it was gossip. It was mob rule; as soon as we decided something about you as a group, or even about each other, it became an unwritten law in Eden.

Mom's penchant for micro-politics had begun in High School as a cheerleader and later as the Mascot for the International Falls Broncos. She wore a huge horse head and purple horse costume and smashed pie in the Principal's face; she was very popular. My shy father was in the crowd the day she was crowned Homecoming Queen, and he jumped up and cheered so hard that he ripped out the backside of his jeans.

Mom was so charismatic. She made friends instantly, with a mix of flirty fun, and serious knowledge about a lot of topics. She laughed easily, and loved surprises, parties, and being the center of attention. She was very self-conscious sometimes, and very intelligent. Her eyes sharpened when she talked seriously, and she had a way of looking away when she negotiated that belied her lack of confidence, especially with men. She had a "phone voice" that was deceptively bubbly. She could turn from screaming, "You kids BEHAVE!" and answer the phone with a flowing "Hellooo!" that sounded like a laughing brook.

She could fake anything that she needed to, and that was the great danger in being close to Mom. Only her inner circle knows this, but she is a master at presentation; you will see what she wants you to see, and know what she wants you to know.

My mom had a very harsh sense of discipline. She claimed to learn that from my Grandpa Bob, but I doubt if he were alive today that he would agree that he taught her that harshness. She strongly believed (as did Dad) that she had the right and the responsibility to spank her children to get them to "behave." A spanking, by my mother's standards, meant 10-20 whacks on the bare butt. In the early years, she used a wooden spoon, or a stick, but by the time the three adopted "Little Kids" were maturing, it was a long, hollow plastic stick. That thing left welts. The spanking was meant to be hard enough to make a child cry. If I did not cry, especially as I got older, the spanking would get more severe and last longer until I did cry - or until her anger was spent, whichever came first. What Mom called "spankings" some might call beatings or canings. When I stopped being affected by the wooden spoon, around age 9, Mom asked Dad to use a 2x4 plank so that I would definitely cry. I did.

If spanking did not seem to work, Mom would use food deprivation, sleep deprivation, humiliation, or belittling; she was intent on "breaking their will," something that Mom fervently believed had to be done with animals and children. Dad supported her "breaking their will" mantra, but only in the early years would he get involved in the discipline himself. He hated conflict.

Early in their marriage, around 1978-1980, she became very angry with Dad when he substitute-taught and, even further back, when he interned in College. Some of his female students would send notes home with him, and she would go ballistic.

I'm not sure why he showed the notes to her, if these girls' sophomoric and misplaced attentions were not of interest to him. She did have a knack for discovering things, so maybe he was afraid not to; or maybe he was terrorizing her emotionally. The result that the two of them created was an admired man and an extremely jealous and angry woman.

When Becky, who was Uncle Rick and Dad's biological sister, found the brothers when I was about 9, Dad was ecstatic. He didn't even know he had a little sister. Younger than he and Rick, Becky had been adopted to a family in southern Minnesota. According to Mom, the day that they got the phone call, Dad and his newly-discovered sister were overly flirtatious, and loved each other a little too much. Admittedly, Mom's later opinions on flirting and sex were very skewed, but when I was 9, I was completely scandalized by his supposed indiscretion.

The first time I felt an awful, twisted feeling in the pit of my stomach was on the way back Up North from meeting Dad's sister, Becky, for the first (and last) time. That twisted gut would later become a major health issue for me, and was a direct result of carrying emotional stress.

Mom was so angry at Dad that they fought all the way home. The trip to meet Becky was a very long way outside of our normal travel circle - which would have ended at Bemidji, about 100 miles away from the Falls. This drive took us all the way down to Pipestone, Minnesota, in the lower corner of the state; it was about a ten hour drive. It could have been exciting, driving through the waving prairies and numerous farming towns that were so different from our North Woods, but it wasn't.

On the way there it was extremely tense, and on the way home Mom shrilled and cried; she made accusations and demanded answers, and Dad mumbled excuses and resisted passively while he drove. I wasn't entirely sure, but she seemed to be accusing him of an inappropriate love for his newly-discovered little sister. I looked out the window, pacified my sisters, and occasionally had a muted scuffle with one of them.

After hours of wrangling, Mom decided that he was not taking her seriously, and she asked to be let out of the car.

I had been trying to keep my little sisters quiet in the back of the car, so as not to get any stray fire; but now my gut was in full alarm. Dad did as she asked, and pulled over. She got out, crying, and walked away. I felt such complete fear and dread that I could not pretend to not be interested in their fight now.

"Where is she going DAD?"

My voice rose at the end and cracked with fear. That was my Mom! She was gone now, as Dad unhappily obeyed her wave to drive off.

"Dad?!" I tried to reason with him. "*Why are we just driving off?!!*" my brain screamed.

"I don't know." was all he would say.

We drove around town - I and my sisters pressing our noses against the windows frantically trying to catch a glimpse of her, sure that she was gone forever.

I couldn't breathe, or think. The random farm town we were in suddenly became dark and foreboding, and I hated it. This would be where I lost my mother forever. Who knew what would happen to her? My imagination was very robust, and I was putting it to the very darkest of uses.

And then Dad spotted her on the steps of the courthouse in Dassel, or Cokato, or whatever small, Minnesota farm town that we were in.

She was weeping into her arms, and he went up to talk to her, while we sat in the car.

After they talked together on the steps for several hours, she got back into the car and the fight continued at a slightly lower level all the way back home.

The next night, at home, I remember hearing loud fighting going on downstairs. We were supposed to be playing in our bedrooms upstairs. Leah was brave enough to sneak down to the bottom of the stairs.

We were hearing Mom's shrill arguments, and Dad's quiet responses.

"WHACK!"

Somebody was hitting somebody. We stared at each other in panic. We fought all the time, but why were THEY?!

Leah came tiptoeing back up wide-eyed. "She has the broom!"

"Whack! WHACK!" Mom was screaming and hitting him.

I never considered that she was abusing him. I wondered what he had done to earn this beating. I assumed that he must have hurt her very badly to make her do this.

And maybe he did. I never found out.

Chapter 11   S-E-X

The nineteenth Winter Olympics were held in Salt Lake City in 2002, and Elizabeth Smart was kidnapped from her home in the same city. The UK mourned the passing of the Queen Mother, Queen Elizabeth, and two snipers killed 10 people and injured 3 in the US capitol, Washington, DC. President George Bush created the Department of Homeland Security.

In South Dakota, Cindy and I dated long-distance from opposite ends of the state, during which time Cindy would often become exasperated with my emotional neediness. She was dealing with her own demons, and had no band-width for the great weight of my processing my new-found world. We met on an old train bridge in Chamberlain, South Dakota, the middle point between Rapid City where Cindy was and Sioux Falls where I was. It was a dream of mine to get engaged on that bridge, and we risked our lives to do that. It was beautiful, but the relationship was not. The roar of freedom, and all of the new experiences, was so loud that I never even began to listen to Cindy's heart. In those times, when she was done helping me process some new thing that probably seemed ludicrous to her, she would say, "I don't want to talk anymore, call Mom."

So I would. And Karen and I would talk through the night if I needed to. Karen was a really good listener, and she would not remember much of our conversations after her Ambien kicked in; I felt really safe to say anything that I wanted. It was a great way to unload some of the awful stuff that I was getting free from.

Karen knew that her daughter was not wanting to talk to me because Cindy was actually out pursuing other guys (and girls). Karen could see the heart-break coming for me, and she began to campaign for me to move out to Rapid City. She would later say that she did not want to try to tell me that Cindy was really not that into me. It was a very kind way to help me through these experiences.

Karen was a very good friend and counselor. She was "disabled" legally, with government help on all of her bills, and that meant that she did not work at all. In fact, she had never worked. She had four kids with four different men, and had always relied on the welfare system to take care of her, even before her car accident in 1994 when her severe whiplash allowed her to claim permanent disability. She was available 24 hours every day to help me, and she focused all of her energy into helping me deal with all of the emotional toxins. It was the kindest thing anyone had done for me up to that point.

The following summer, I did move to Rapid City to be closer to Cindy and Karen. Cindy and I were engaged, and I was eagerly awaiting our wedding day. My parents were still refusing to have anything to do with us, and Cindy was becoming tired of waiting to get their approval.

I bought an old tour bus before I left Sioux Falls, and Cindy and I were planning to live and travel in it. She got very excited about the bus, and when I moved to Rapid City, the plan was for me to live in it at the tourist attraction where I had a job, and for both of us to finish it inside and live in it after we were married. The night that I arrived in Rapid City with the bus Cindy met me at a truck stop, and had been sending me teasing messages all day. I was hot and bothered. When she climbed onto "our" bus, she was uncharacteristically vulnerable and clearly horny.

We ended up on the bed, and she was on top of me. It was a simple motion to complete our union physically, and she was doing everything she could to make it very easy to slide inside. I stopped her.

"I REALLY want to," I said, with ragged breath.

"But I don't want to get you pregnant before we get married, and I don't want you to regret it happening this way."

I was committed to doing things right. And Cindy may have felt scorned.

Not long after I settled into life in Rapid City, I could sense that we were not ok. We fought constantly. I was very clingy and possessive, and she resisted by disappearing and lying to me.

One day that spring, in front of the storage units where she kept her stuff, she handed me the engagement ring back. We had been fighting again, but I was shocked; I was not ready for this extreme reaction.

I dropped to my knees, crying.

"Don't make me beg! I love you!" I sobbed.

She looked angry. And distressed. She often struggled to say what she was thinking.

"I love you too, as much as my hard little heart can love," she said.

"But it's just not going to work." I knew she was right.

She left me there, with the ring in my hand. Broken.

After that breakup, I went out to the piece of property where my bus was parked, and I melted inside. It was not dramatic, or violent. I was entirely alone. My parents would be thrilled to hear that we had broken up, and they would welcome me with open arms. But I would not go back. I cried some, but mostly I just stared at the inside of the bus walls and thought. And didn't think. It was a lot of pain, and at the same time I wanted to learn something from it, to try to make it meaningful.

It felt like a part of me quit fighting. I did not drink, or medicate in any other way. I just spent about two weeks trying to cope with my new reality, and to learn the lesson.

I have come to a great deal of peace with Cindy now, though I have not spoken to her since. I have realized that I still love and respect her for some things that she did in my life. I also have accepted that she wasn't able to love me in the romantic way that I had wanted, nor did I love her without condition. I have the most amazing love now, and I am eternally grateful that Cindy broke up with me. I did not feel that way at the time.

I was still reeling a bit, but determined to move on, when I went over to the little blue house on East St Patrick Street where Karen lived and where Cindy might still be living. I was taking a chance; Karen welcomed me. It had been weeks, and she said that she had been afraid, and almost certain, that she would never see me again. Cindy, it turned out, had moved to the East Coast to be with a woman that she had fallen in love with. Karen had sobbed for days when Cindy came out to her as a lesbian.

Karen and I were the only close friends or family that either of us had right at that point. At least that either of us were accepting. So I visited often, and we supported each other. We became very deep friends very quickly.

One day, in the middle of the day, some time after Cindy had moved away, kneeling by the recliner that she lived in, I kissed Karen on the mouth. We were both a little shocked, but it got very steamy very fast. We kissed for two hours, as I recall. Eventually, I wanted more.

"You want to fuck," she said, shocked.

I will never forget what I said next.

"Is there any way that you can get pregnant?" I asked.

"I had a hysterectomy," she said. "That means I don't even have a uterus anymore."

Yes, I wanted to fuck.

And I clearly did not want to have children with her. Not an early sign of complete commitment.

Sex turned out to be not what I expected. But at the age of 29, I was finally not a virgin anymore. I couldn't have explained why it was not what I expected - until years later. But at the time, I felt that it was still amazing, and I was thrilled to be in love.

I remember one other small detail from my relationship with Karen that now stands out very large. At one point, before we were officially married, I asked if she was "saved."

It was as if somehow she was good enough for me to fuck, but she might not pass muster spiritually. It was the first of an endless string of conditions to my love.

She did not like the conversation, or the pressure that I was putting on her, and though she finally gave in, her being "saved" properly soon led to me needing her to meet any number of other requirements that I felt were important - so I could love her.

We were married anyway, and my mom and dad had another reason to write me off. My family and I had reconnected after Cindy left, but their attempts to leverage me back into the fold would not work on me anymore, and they soon found more reasons to stop communicating with me. They have always been able to find a reason to keep me away, now that I am a threat to the bubble on Eden Road; and more importantly, a threat to the bubble that is still the family cult.

I was married to Karen for 8 years. She was 17 years older than I was. I fed her, clothed her, bathed her, and watched TV with her. We went to the adult store together. I explored anal sex with her, (both giving and receiving, using toys) and we discussed "swinging." We were both determined to break any taboos that we grew up with and to decide for ourselves what we liked. I also learned that I was not a gay man, and that I did not like anal sex with a woman either. I was far too jealous to be a swinger; we never even attempted it.

I was finally "trying everything" as the Shakira song says, and I was learning who I was. Karen did not care if I explored Internet Porn, and we did it together. She did not expect me to report to her if I watched it on my own; I reveled in the free feeling and I learned what I liked. I discovered that I was an extremely straight man, who loved shorter, curvier girls with round bottoms and big breasts. I also tended to like red-heads. There were a great many really nasty things on porn sites that I found I could not enjoy. I would never have known that for sure if I had not been permissioned to learn it.

Karen, as a mentor, demonstrated for me that there is a reason that mentors generally do not have sex with their mentees. It is an abuse of a relationship of trust, and it does not end well. Karen became much less interested in sex after the first two years, and it was not long after we were joined for the first time that I began to become aware of the challenges that she dealt with. She told me that she had multiple personality disorder, and I immediately felt that I should help her with that. I had no idea what it was. I could write an entire book about the experience of the next couple of years.

Her personalities had different names, voices, and energies. I could tell which one was there by looking at her face. She would "flick" (her word) between "parts;" parts like Andrea Wellington, who was 2 years old, brilliant, and was the part of her that did all of the learning. Andrea knew Mandarin, studied law, science, and anything else she could study. Felicia was a bitch by her own description, and she was the one who handled all of the pain (there had been a lot of it in Karen's life). Felicia loved sex, and had been the one that realized that I wanted to "fuck," (Felicia swore like a sailor, though Karen never did).

Semae was the oldest part, and at first we just called her The Guardian. The other parts saw her as a trash can, because she had all of the memories. She was the wisest part; and she controlled which part was "out." We discovered a new part that was a man, and Karen named it Joshua, which seemed very odd to me. I insisted that I help Karen put all of her parts back into one, and that took two years. Karen did that for me, I realized later, because I had immediately assumed that being in pieces was not healthy.

It was extremely humbling to learn that when a woman loved me, she would literally turn herself into anything that I wanted her to be. I was not responsible with that power.

It would have been better if we had not put Karen back together. I was very much not qualified to be dealing with advanced psychosis like hers, and I was still trying to fix everything for everyone, as I had practiced with my mother. In Karen's case, it was harmful to her. Her pieces had helped her cope and, after a short time of being all in one piece, the real stresses of being married to me crushed her and she shattered into pieces again.

This time, I was not allowed to know about her inner workings. I had said too many hurtful, mean, insensitive things, and she no longer felt safe with me. I did not blame her; I had learned early how to destroy someone with my words, and I was still very good at using those weapons.

I cried for two days that weekend that I realized that I could say something that I could never take back and that would destroy forever someone that I professed to love. In my family, that idea had never been considered; but my painful new awareness permanently changed the way that I lashed people with my verbal skills.

It was too late for Karen and I. It was the beginning of the end of our marriage, even though we would make a great pretense for years. In 2006 I began two years of online research from Sioux Falls, South Dakota, which culminated in Karen and I moving out to Colorado in 2008. Once in our new home, I took a job as a Union Electrician, and was later elected Business Manager of the Electrician's Union, Local 969, in Grand Junction. Karen and I drifted further and further away from each other in our hearts. But I am getting ahead of myself.

In the beginning, when Karen and I got engaged, she was still fully present, and doing her best to help me with my past. I continued to process through memories and beliefs that I had created while I was in the Carpenter Family cult. The most difficult memory was a six-year-long horror story that happened to my sister, Susanna.

Chapter 12   Susanna

It was 2003. In April, the human Genome Project was completed, with scientists successfully mapping over 99% of human DNA, including 20,000 individual genes and base pairs. It had been a 13-year-long project, with far-reaching implications for the relatively new science of genomics. Also that year, the Department of Homeland Security officially began operations, Lance Armstrong won his fifth Tour De France, and President George W. Bush announced aboard the carrier USS *Abraham Lincoln* that major US operations in Iraq were over. *Lord Of The Rings; Return of the King, Bruce Almighty,* and *The Last Samurai* were on the big screen, and a hiker in Moab, Utah cut off his own arm to save his life and escape certain death in a hiking accident. His story would become a book and a movie in later years, but in 2003 it made for great water-cooler discussions. Would you do that if you had to? Could you?

I was driving along the road in Sioux Falls, South Dakota, in a piece-of-crap Mitsubishi. It was ready for the scrap heap; but it was still more dependable and better on gas than the Oldsmobile that I left Eden Road with; the $1500 car that sold for $700 my first month in Sioux Falls. I was glad to be rid of it.

I was on the phone with Karen, processing through things that I remembered from my past. A casual comment brought a buried memory to my mind.

I had to pull the car over.

My heart was in my throat.

My pulse was racing.

I said, "Hold on..." as I tossed the phone onto the dash. I opened my door and put my head out. I thought I was going to throw up.

As I was adapting to life outside of Eden Road, and the little bubble that we had maintained for decades, I began to see memories and situations from the past differently. The way the average human might. Someone who had not been brainwashed into the Carpenter Family Singers. Someone who did not have my original belief system. Maybe someone more balanced and healthy. This was one of those memories.

In an instant, as I replayed it, I saw the situation for what it was.

A real life horror story.

And I saw my mother the way that the rest of the world would see her.

In the news. In jail.

A bitter, angry, sallow faced woman with a heart so hard that I could not know it, and a mind so twisted that she didn't even know anymore what was real and what was her own fabrication.

She had almost killed my little sister, Susanna. The one from Belize. And I had done nothing to stop her.

It was this memory that had me almost retching on the side of the road when I recalled it.

When Susanna came to us in that blizzard from Minneapolis, she was 3 months old. She had a dissociative disorder that can happen with adopted children, as a result of being rejected by her birth mother. I learned about this much later; that as humans we feel everything that happens, even in the womb, by the energy that it carries with it. And Baby Susanna had been deeply affected by the rejection of her biological mother. On our little farm, in Morgan, MN, we had never heard of this phenomenon.

Mom decided that Susanna had an evil spirit.

Susanna, at age three months, and worse at 6 months, was a very difficult baby. All she wanted was to lie naked in her crib. She REALLY did not want to be touched or held, and she whined about everything. Her crying had no logic to it. And Mom's harsh discipline had no affect. This infuriated Mom.

Mom decided to "discipline it out of her." She would spank Susanna for crying until she was black and blue from the middle of her back to her ankles. And Susanna was brown, so dark spots should have been harder to see. But these were rainbow-colored and welted. I can see them to this day and I shudder. That was not the worst of it.

When spanking did not work, Mom would deprive Susanna of sleep or food, intent on "breaking her will."

And then there was bath time. Susanna hated baths. She whined the whole time. Mom hated whining, so she would spank Susanna. Then Susanna would cry and often fart, or poop in the tub. Mom saw this as defiance, and that was almost Susanna's death. Mom started battling this constant whining by putting Susanna's head under the tub spout with the water running in her face. The water was cold... very cold. Mom's term for this discipline was "Cold Water."

This happened many different times, but one stands out in my memory. Mom had started the bath before a concert, and started early. It seemed that the more important it was for a smooth concert preparation - the more whining there would be from Susanna.

Just getting Susanna undressed resulted in whining; it was obvious that this time would not be smooth. Mom addressed her sternly, "Susanna, STOP IT."

Susanna just got louder. She wasn't even in the tub yet.

I looked away, walked to a different part of the house, and tried to ignore the building battle.

But the bathroom was central to the house, and as I did my own prep for the gig, I had to repeatedly pass them. Susanna was in the tub now, and howling. Mom was howling back.

Mom had ramped up quickly to fight mode. Susanna was on her back, face up, under the faucet.

As Susanna gasped for air, it was much harder to cry and whine. But she did, now with a terror added to her whining.

"Susanna, do you want Cold Water?!" Mom demanded.

"No! No! No!" Susanna tried to protest in abject fear; but she couldn't stop her whining so she almost always got the cold water once it was threatened.

Her eyes were wide open under the flowing tap… on full blast. She never closed her eyes. She left them wide open. It was the stuff of nightmares.

Susanna had not stopped, so Mom took the wash rag and stuffed it in her mouth, making it impossible for Susanna to make anything except a choking, gurgling sound. She was thrashing, and Mom was screaming, "Are you going to STOP? I command you in the name of Jesus to STOP! You have no authority here, SATAN! Are you going to STOP Susanna? OH, you want to fight with me?" This last was said with an almost competitive tone. It was getting hard to tell if she was addressing Jesus, Satan, or Susanna.

More thrashing, spanking, and gurgling.

I was 17 at the time, and I was scared to DEATH. Mom was only 5'7", and I was 6'5", with an athletic build. I might have done something to stop her.

But I had been scared of Mom for years. So I watched my very dominant sister, Leah, fall into little pieces because she tried to do what I could not even consider.

"MOM!" Leah had stepped part-way into the bathroom. "Mom, you've got to STOP!"

This last was louder to be heard over the choking and shrieking of the 1-year-old in the tub. Mom looked up, in a rage.

"WHAT? LEAH? What do you WANT me to do with THIS?" she gestured disdainfully into the tub.

Leah stopped her charge into the fray. She paused, but went doggedly on.

"I don't know.

Mom.

But this is WRONG! You are going to kill her!"

Leah was always stronger than I was. Until what happened next. Mom went for her throat emotionally. She took the naked, dripping baby out of the tub and offered her to Leah.

"TAKE her then!" Leah stepped back involuntarily. "No, Mom, I...."

Mom thrust screaming Susanna out towards Leah again.

"You take her. I'm SURE that you know what to do much better than me." This last dripped with sarcasm.

And Leah may have done better than Mom with Susanna, but she did not believe that about herself. I watched my proud, courageous, 16-year-old best friend crumble into a million pieces in front of me. My beautiful, tall, blonde sister would never be the same. To my eyes and heart, it felt like she picked up some awful darkness that day. I know that the powerful, dominant part of her nature wanted to take the baby, and call Mom's bluff. I know that she wanted to do what she knew in her soul was right. But she did not. She had no network, no job, no idea how to raise a baby. And so she wilted back. Mom turned back to her abuse. Leah became, like me, a regretful accomplice to the crimes that my mom was committing on little children. I give her credit; at least she had tried to do something about it.

On the side of a sunny South Dakota road in my Mitsubishi I was sweating and crying and praying. I didn't want to see my lovely mother this way.

But the authorities would. Maybe they could stop her. Those kids were 8, 10, and 10 and as I sat in my car in Sioux Falls, I knew that I had to do something. How could I possibly have just left and not ever done anything to stop her?!! I was feeling extremely guilty, and angry, and helpless.

I wrote a letter, later that week, to Brown County Social Services, because I heard through the grapevine that my parents were now taking in foster children.

WHAT?! This was beyond belief. Why?! How...?! My mother had no business caring for innocent children.

I wrote a letter warning the county that things were not what they seemed on Eden Road. But my mother was, and is, a master at covering things up. Putting on a smile and a professional phone voice as she tells you that you are wrong, you are not seeing what you think you are seeing.

Silence. Keep the secrets.

Denial. You did not see what you thought you saw.

Isolation. Don't talk to anyone who may know the family about what you saw; don't talk to anyone in the family itself, for that matter.

And I did exactly that. I ran away for ten years - avoiding contact with every. Single. Family. Member. And friend. I did exactly what I was trained to do.

Dad knew every bit of what was happening and would never fight Mom, even if he did think that she was being too harsh. He hated conflict.

None of us ever spoke of Mom's abuse to her or each other, that I know of, until my sister Sarah and her husband Mark returned from Africa in 2013.

Susanna continued to be abused in ways that Mom deemed appropriate until she was roughly six years old. The whining was still happening at bedtime.

One night when Susanna was 6, Mom told her to go put her pajamas on and get ready for bed. Susanna started to whine; Mom said something like, "I don't want to hear it Susanna," and Susanna went upstairs to put her PJs on.

When she came back downstairs to where Mom was doing paperwork Susanna said, "I'm getting too old for this aren't I, Mom?" and Mom said, "Yes, you are Susanna." Susanna nodded and she never did it again.

After I left the group, and especially after my letter that exposed what I knew about her methods to the authorities at Brown County, Mom and Dad made sure that I never spoke to Susanna as a child. I chatted with her briefly one time when she happened to pick up the phone at the Farm on Eden Road. They were quite upset about that chance interaction, even though I was never going to mention anything about her abusive past to an 11-year-old.

Chapter 13
Healing From the Cult

Immediately after I left home, I asked two respected men in my life if I was possessed - as Mom had suggested on the day that I left. Both men had worked on people with "evil spirits" and had reportedly cast out demons as part of their ministry or healing profession. Both of them knew our family quite well. One of these men wept at my request, because he could see the weapon that Mom's accusation had become in my heart. Both of the men that I asked assured me that, with their extensive spiritual experience, I was definitely not possessed.

Several books and articles that I read after I left home clearly defined a "cult" by certain behaviors. These behaviors can be found in some very surprising, ordinary places. Maybe at work. Very likely at church. It is our human reaction to the free will that the other humans around us are born with.

Group think, mob rule, decision by committee. Individual freedoms being absorbed by the good of the group. Tight restrictions on having sex, especially if you are not a leader in the group. A core set of beliefs that are obsessively adhered to, regardless of science or even clear results to the contrary. The big hammer that keeps the cult working is what will happen to me, the individual, if I go against the will or laws of the group.

It is called shunning. It is used very often in places that we would not think of as cults.

Here is an example of the way that shunning works today, using my experience as an example.

After leaving, my family made it clear that until I repented of my decisions that were contrary to their wishes or judgement (stop dating Cindy), I would not be spoken to or welcomed in any way by anyone in the group. Mom made sure that I got fired from my dream job in Christian radio, because she knew everyone in that Christian community, and they played by many of the same rules that she was using in our family.

All Mom had to do was tell them that I was having premarital sex with Cindy and doing drugs and drinking heavily; even though I have never been drunk in my life, to this day, and I have never done any drugs, and Cindy and I never actually had intercourse. But the Christian community there was quick to believe the accusations from someone who was "in" their cult, if you will.

In the extended Pullar family, Mom continues to this day to spread lies and exaggerate "her side" of the story to their little circle. Many of the aunts and uncles do not know what to believe anymore. These are classic shunning techniques.

The family cult being threatened by my leaving made it necessary for Mom and Dad to put up an even-taller, invisible wall between the Carpenter Family and the "outside world." It has always been there, and it keeps their way of life "safe."

I am now on the outside of that wall, along with Sarah and Josiah. I choose to believe that healing has come to us, and that it is meant for every family member.

My heart aches for Josiah's sweet, sunny soul, which was darkened by the pain of rejection and abuse. Mom, who was used to my style of learning and easy grasp of home-schooling, had struggled with Leah's dyslexia, and really became angry when Josiah had exhibited signs of a learning disability. She would try to help him, but by that time she was completely engrossed in the music business, and had no bandwidth for his needs.

She would pound on his head with her closed fist, one hit for each syllable, shouting at him, "WHY. ARE. YOU. SO. STU-PID?" while tears streamed down his face.

He is not, in fact, stupid, and now, in his quest to be the best Bull Rider he can be, he loves self-improvement books. He tells me stories of his own about the abuses that he suffered after I left, and they were awful. I will let him tell them in his own time, if he chooses to. I have apologized to him for leaving him and our siblings without doing anything to change the situation that was causing him such unnecessary pain. We are good friends to this day, and connect often. He is quite a student and has brilliant instincts.

My sister Sarah, who wrote the opening note for this book, has been a very strong source of support in writing this book. As I have laid bare some of my most embarrassing choices, and darkest moments, it might have been easy to sink into the negative thinking and self-trashing that can go with reliving my mistakes. Sarah has always been there, even at the very early days, to illustrate that making mistakes is ok, and to let me know that sharing them is brave and may help others with their mistakes. My favorite story about handling mistakes is about Sarah.

When my family and I were on stage singing, probably around 1999, Sarah had a very strong vocal part at the end of a particularly stirring song near the end of every show. It was a sort of climax to the performance. One night, as the band reached a point near the end, she accidentally lost her place and sang her part very loudly into the wrong spot in the song. Since no one else was joining her, it was extremely obvious that she had made a colossal mistake.

What she did next was brilliant. She had an opportunity to be embarrassed, and go deep into beating herself up. But she did not do that. In the next ten seconds, as the place that she was SUPPOSED to be coming in rolled around, she grabbed her microphone, took a giant goose-step to the center and front of the stage, and hit her note with a very exaggerated gusto. The audience roared, and she made an impact on me forever. In ten seconds, Sarah had processed through guilt and embarrassment and got to……freedom. Freedom from what others would think of her. It gave her a clear head and clean heart to even enjoy the humor of the moment and maximize the effect of her vocal crescendo.

That day Sarah was acting on some advice that Dad gave us very early in our careers.

On a particular evening, at one of our first shows, one of the girls had made a small mistake on stage, and she had become so embarrassed and angry about it, that it derailed the whole show.

Dad, addressing us afterward, ages 10-15, asked a question.

"Why do you guys think people go to a rodeo?"

I shrugged. The girls looked around. "To see horses and cows and cowboys?"

"Maybe," he said, "but I think the real reason is that they want to see somebody get bucked off and maybe stepped on."

We stared, not following.

"That is exactly why they go to your live shows: they want to see you get bucked off and how you will handle it!"

We were beginning to see.

"So next time you make a mistake, laugh it off, smile, move on; don't worry about it. Odds are they didn't even notice it, but even if they did, it's exactly your mistakes that make your shows unique!"

This advice really took the pressure off of us, and in an odd way, I believe, made this book possible. Nobody is perfect, every family is dysfunctional on some level, and by talking about what didn't work, maybe we can get to what DOES work!

As I healed from the cult and our mistakes as a group, my sister Sarah and my brother Josiah came alongside me and helped me deal with the past. Sometimes, just sharing stories and releasing the memories is enough; and sometimes, it really helps to have someone who was there with you to validate your experience. Here is a memory of Sarah's from those days, printed with her permission; in fact, she sent this to me on the eve of printing, because she wanted to get it out.

"I remember multiple times with Josiah and Susanna that Mom would beat them with the plastic stick until they fell down to their knees and she would have them by the arm and be yelling at them, "Stand up! You stand up!" and she would continue to beat them until they stood up. I believe she saw their falling to the ground as defiance or resistance ...trying to evade the 'spanking.'

I remember Susanna would fart or even poop sometimes and Mom would yell at her, 'You are disgusting! Don't you dare do that!' It was so horrible. I remember taking Kila (Tequila ...the little Mexican dog with worms that Joshua named :) on a walk across a soybean field when we were preparing to sing once at an old folks home in the middle of nowhere in Minnesota. Mom was beating the crap out of Susanna or Josiah (I don't remember which one) and I left for a walk with the dog because I couldn't handle being in the bus any more. I remember looking across that endless field wanting to keep walking. But where would I go? What would I do? I was 20 something. It was about 30 minutes till concert time. I walked back to the bus and we did another concert. All smiles and autographs. I hated that day."

Sarah, thank you. I cannot tell you what your support has meant to me, and how your one lone voice from those early days - who remembers what I do - has kept me sane and going forward. Hugs.

Sarah and Mark returned in 2012 from living as missionaries in Uganda, where Mark was a school principal for 7 years. In 2013, they came to the States with their three children; Seth, Jodie, and Megan, and we met them in Denver with our two youngest, Nathan and Tasha. Mark Williams is a tall, good looking Canadian man who is emotionally healthy and spiritually strong, and has been so good for Sarah, and me, and our family. When Mark married into the family he did his best to join the family as in-laws typically do. When he began to experience the cultish behaviours of the Carpenter family he pushed back, resisting the patterns he knew were wrong. And he paid for it.

In a very short period of time he began to be treated like an outsider; marginalized, ignored, and targeted. He does not accept the cult's guidelines, and I respect him for it. Every year, as we tour, Candy and I go to the Williams' home in British Columbia and laugh and love and stay up late playing Settlers of Catan and watching movies and having epic croquet battles on the lawn. It feels so good to have family in my life again.

Sarah and I chat regularly, and she and Mark have been a huge source of support. If you are alone in something like this, my heart is with you, because it is easy to think that you are the crazy one. Sarah, Josiah, and I would like you to know that you are not. I say, be you. Wildly, passionately, rebelliously, you.

Dad is retired now, with salt and pepper hair and walks with a stoop, but continues to work for Mom as a paid employee at the *House of Lights* on Eden Road.

Leah developed a 'female problem" and gained a bunch of weight. It felt to me that this resulted from her deep unhappiness. Leah is married now, and has adopted three children. I don't know what her "female problems" were or are, but I know that she appears miserable still. And she is repeating Mom's pattern of destroying her spouse.

The last conversation that I had with her ended when I confronted her about belittling and complaining about her husband Kalvin - whom she married soon after the music group closed. On that particular call I stopped her haranguing of Kalvin and gave her a choice; either divorce him and complain to me about what a jerk he was, or stay with him and tell me what is awesome about him. She has never spoken to me again, and Kalvin warned me at a family wedding recently to stay away from his wife. Leah is apparently close to Mom and Dad today, I believe, although none of them who are inside the bubble tell me anything anymore.

As I poured out these memories on my laptop, I wondered if Susanna was alright. I had seen her at Grandpa Bob's funeral, where Mom had continued to shun me, my wife, and step daughter. Susanna had waited until Mom was not around and then approached me and went on quite cheerfully about her now-adult life. She was 27 years old, and very successful, far away from the family geographically.

On the advice of my good friend, Lance McMahan, a sponsor of this book, I contacted Susanna through Facebook. I was deeply concerned that she knew nothing about her childhood abuse. Our exchange was through Messenger, and happened in January of 2019, as I was writing this book. I happened to be within a five-hour-drive of where she was living, and thought we could get together to talk about what I was writing. She was quick to question what the purpose of the meeting would be, and suggested that if it was about "past extreme treatment of me as a child" that I should save myself the trip.

I texted that it was indeed, and that I wanted to clear up some things that had been on my conscience for some time. As if she had been groomed for this conversation, and without even questioning what new information I may have for her, she became very defensive of Mom, and said that Mom had only been acting in her (Susanna's) best interest, and that Susanna had known about the "treatment" for a long time and that Mom and she were on good terms. "I'm glad someone loved me enough to do that for me," she texted. She said that I should just drop it.

I tried to gently suggest that maybe I could just get it off of my chest, even if she had heard it all before. Susanna became very militant in her defense of Mom, and when I could not agree with her assessments of what happened in the past, she ended the messaging.

I am not at all confident that she has ever heard any of the details as I have just written them, because my mother is competent at downplaying things that might make the Carpenter Family look bad. And Mom has hidden herself under the bubble at Eden Road, which now extends to anywhere her remaining loyal children live. I hope and pray that if Susanna reads this and has a negative reaction, that she seeks professional help.

Jeremiah has maintained a relationship with me in a similar way to Susanna. When Mom is present, he shuns me. When Mom is not looking, he can be quite friendly and pleasant.

Melita is Mom and Dad's book keeper. She has maintained a very great distance from me. I am not sure that her husband, Ken, knows the details of Mom's abusiveness. I don't think that he would allow Mom to watch his kids the way she does if he knew that she is not stable. He has tried to voice his intuitive concerns, from what I understand, but Melita has apparently stonewalled him.

I have made repeated connections with Mom and Dad, and each time, even though our relationship is re-established briefly, there will be a period of testing, to see if I am complying with their demands. There has always been a new and different reason given for disconnection.

Once, they suddenly decided it was because my wife and I slept and lived together before marriage. Once it was because they did not believe I was actually "saved" by their standards. Once because I was no longer reading the Bible regularly. Once, Mom and I had a ferocious argument because I disagreed with her harsh views and defended the idea that gay people should be loved rather than shunned. She felt that loving them meant insisting that they "get help" to be "cured."

I will admit, I have known each time that they would re-shun me. I willingly allowed myself to be shunned, sticking up for my truth, instead of submitting to their rule on the matter.

They would say that it is I who chose to offend them and thus chose to be rejected.

I will never again submit my free will to a group of people and their demands on my behavior and my beliefs. And I will not expect my kids to do that either. I seek groups that support and hold me accountable and give me feedback; albeit without the threat of shunning, and with emphasis on every person's free will. I have overcome the fear of my failings, and the fear of human failings in general. I believe that things are improving, and that we are learning. The future is beautiful.

Chapter 14
God Hates Divorce

In 2010, it was the year of Facebook. And the Ipad was a smash hit. "*Lost*" was ending, and *Jersey Shore* was continuing. Taylor Swift was sweeping the awards, and at the World Cup in South Africa vuvuzelas and the United States were both new and loud on the world soccer scene.

And in Colorado, I asked Karen for a divorce. It happened very quickly following two conversations. The first was at the foot of Karen's recliner, where I implored her to get out of her chair and go out with me and do SOMETHING. She spent all of her waking moments on the computer or watching and recording cable TV programs. I was making really good money, and had funded several different types of business opportunities for her, but she had as yet never actually decorated a wedding cake, or created a website, or finished a saleable craft. Or developed a functioning, paying, You-Tube Channel.

These were all things that I had sunk many thousands of dollars into for equipment and programs, only to have her OxyContin addiction or Ambien use become her excuse to not make any use of them. I was begging her, on my knees.

"Let's go do something! Anything! Let's get out of here and do something fun!"

I brushed at tears. "I can't stay here and die with you!"

I was gaining weight because my office job was not physical, and every night after I made supper was spent watching TV until I couldn't stay awake any longer - at which point I would crawl upstairs and into my bed, which Karen had never even been in.

Before falling asleep, I would probably watch some porn, and masturbate my stress away. Karen was just glad that I wasn't expecting her to have sex with me.

She almost never left the chair. And she left the apartment so rarely that the guys at work teased me that she didn't actually exist. They claimed that "Karen" was just a cover story, since they had never met her, and that I was in fact a closeted gay man. I took the ribbing good-naturedly, but there was a little pain in the truth of it.

In front of Karen's recliner, I waited for an answer. It took a long time. She didn't even look me in the eye. She didn't say anything. She shrugged.

My heart was broken by her indifference, but I took my tears upstairs. I was clearly going to have to move on without her, if I wanted to be more healthy and active. I was just a paycheck and a cook and a home health aide for her now. There was no heart left in our marriage.

Some days later, I was in the office at Bemis Electric, dropping off a few pieces of paperwork from the Union Hall. The Office Manager at Bemis Electric, Candy, had worked for me at the Hall after I had worked as her service guy for a couple of years at Bemis.

We worked really well together, and her boss, Lee Bemis, had been kind to both of us, allowing her to spend twenty hours per week at the Hall, straightening out our books and procedures in the office. She was a huge blessing in my new position, and during the downturn that hit the valley hard in 2010, she and Lee welcomed her extra hours at the Union Hall. It was a win/win. We spent many hours working together to clean the mess up at the Hall, but never once engaged in the least bit of hanky panky. I was faithful, and she had no interest in a married man, though she was playing the field of single men.

Candy and her daughters Autumn and Tasha helped Karen and I move into our second place in Colorado, a farm apartment. They were some of the very few people in Grand Junction who actually knew Karen, and Karen thought they were great. She loved anyone who would do things for her; she expected it, in fact.

Back in the office at Bemis Electric, Candy was asking me how I was. She had finished her work at the Hall for me some months earlier, and I hadn't seen her in a while. She was a good friend, and the answer I gave her took her back.

I was surprised to have tears in my eyes, and instead of what I thought I might say to catch her up on small newsy bits, I unloaded the whole story of how I had asked Karen to get out of the house and pursue better health and then how my heart broke with her shrug.

Candy was clearly uncomfortable. Until that moment, she believed that Karen and I were madly in love, and that we had, in fact, a model marriage. She had no idea what to say. She expressed her condolences that things were not going well for me, and I left her office rather brusquely. I sat in my car for ten minutes or more, trying to understand what had just happened.

I had just shared my heart with a girl that I worked with, and she had listened, while my "wife" had simply shrugged. I knew my marriage was over. I had no idea that I would be dating Candy in a whirlwind turn of events, but I knew for a fact that I was no longer married to Karen.

I believe that God hates divorce, as the Bible says, because of all of the pain and breaking that happens on the way to the final legal documentation. I believe that He hates when people have sex and decide to commit to someone that they will have to ultimately separate from in the end. I believe He hates it because He hates to see my heart hurt. Some people have used that verse to further bludgeon people who have already seen all of the pain of a divorce. I think it's better not to attack anyone with any verse of the Bible. I don't think that's what it is meant for.

I also know from personal experience that as painful as divorce is, sometimes it is the healthiest and most positive choice for both people involved.

When I left the farm apartment for the last time, never to see Karen again, I searched for words to find closure. I did not hate her. I felt very little for her. I was beginning to realize that I had simply gone from rescuing my mother and taking on her victim story to taking on Karen and rescuing her.

"You need to get help, Karen. I don't hate you at all. I know that you need some professional help, and I was never qualified to be that help. I hope that you find it."

I walked out the door.

When my relationship with Cindy ended, I had mourned, and I felt very alone. When I walked out of Karen's door, I felt nothing but relief. Our relationship had been disintegrating since before we said our vows. And neither of us had asked for any outside help. By the time I left, we had created such mistrust and pain that there there was nothing left to repair.

After filing the divorce paperwork, I asked Candy for advice, because I remembered that she had been divorced.

"Did you get an attorney?" she asked.

"Oh, no," I said, "We are still friends; we both signed the agreement that I printed out online. I'm sure we don't need to go that route; it's called an amicable divorce."

Candy didn't argue with me, but I could see that she wasn't buying it. And I wasn't listening.

She was right though.

Karen became very bitter very quickly, and though I did not move out for a couple of weeks, it was definitely NOT amicable. It was a six month legal ordeal.

I ended up getting an attorney, whose first words to me were, "You're screwed."

I gulped. "Why?"

"You make really good money, and she is 'disabled,'" he said. "The judge will give her everything. But I like you, and I will do my best to help you."

It was underwhelming, but I would take any help I could get, even if I had to pay him handsomely to tell me that I was screwed.

After actually meeting Karen at an introductory hearing, as she rolled into the courtroom in her electric chair (she could walk, but heavily played up her "disability") my attorney started giggling. He was not the sort of man who giggles often.

"What is so funny?" I asked.

"She won't get an attorney. She is a rolling lie. No one in town will touch her case, even though she qualifies for pro bono help. Judges hate people who lie to them."

He was right. Karen lied about $7500 cash that I gave her. She lied about her disability. She lied about whether or not she could requalify for her disability compensation. The whole courtroom caught our collective breath when she stated that I had been bathing her before our divorce, and she had not had a shower since I left 5 months earlier. That was likely true.

The judge decreed that I pay Karen's rent for 1 year. That was all. It was a huge win for me, and for justice. It felt like a hollow victory. I had lost a friend and mentor, and have never heard from her again. After all of the pain that we had inflicted on each other, it was for the best.

I can see why God hates divorce.

Chapter 15   Candy

It was 2011, and the Arab Spring was taking the Middle East by storm. Osama Bin Laden was killed in hiding by a US military team, and an earthquake and Tsunami did terrible damage to the Fukushima nuclear power plant in Japan, leaving roughly 23,000 dead or missing, and triggering a nuclear crisis that would affect the entire planet for a very long time. *Game of Thrones* debuted its first season, as did *Shameless*. The second half of *Harry Potter and the Deathly Hallows, The Help, Hangover Part 2, The Green Lantern*, and *Bridesmaids* were on the big screen, just to name a few.

In Fruita, Colorado, just outside Grand Junction, Candy and I had been seeing each other on several evenings after work, as it became apparent that I was about to be in the legal battle of my life with my soon-to-be ex-wife over my future fortunes. I was scared, and Candy was kind enough not to remind me that she had tried to warn me. I had a new apartment, and was about to move into it. My stuff was already there. Animosity at the farm apartment that Karen and I had been sharing was getting intense. It didn't feel safe for either of us.

On the opposite front, I had been experiencing an odd sensation of wanting to kiss Candy, as we talked through the ins and outs of the next steps in the legal battle. We had become such good friends in the three years of working together, but I had never looked at her as a lover. Now I couldn't see anything else.

I told her I loved her. On May 30th, 2011, she leaned across her truck console and kissed me. I went home with her soon after that kiss, and we have never stopped kissing. It was very fast; a mere two weeks after I asked Karen for a divorce. We both were aware that we were breaking every good relationship rule out there. Work relationships don't work. Rebounds don't work. Friendships end when people become lovers. People are bound to assume hanky-panky. New relationships are best to wait until the divorce is final.

But we did not wait. In an odd way, it was the first clean and honest relationship that we had each had. It was hot and heavy right away; and 8 years later it still is. That girl is proof to me that Someone loves me and has seen all of the struggles and pain - and that I have been blessed beyond what I deserve. She is simply amazing.

The first night that I had sex with Candy, I was blown away. She was my type, in every way. Curves that melted my jeans off; breasts that were so perfect, I later confessed to her that I thought they were fake. But much more than that, when I made love to her, she fucked me back. I had never experienced that.

I finally was catching up to what my heart knew was possible back when I was 13 rubbing on my bed sheets in the basement, or when I was 15 and getting off to romance novels, or when I was kissing a lesbian and wondering what intercourse would feel like, or when I was having sex with a woman who just wanted me to be satisfied, but did not seem to enjoy the act herself.

After a couple of months of torrid love making, I told Candy that I wanted to take her on our first official date. She agreed happily.

I was very nervous, in my shiny silver suit that she had helped me pick out some months before. I needed one for work, and I did not trust my own sense of style. Hers was impeccable.

As we enjoyed the meal at Johnny Carino's, our favorite spot, I fiddled with my fork.

She knew me pretty well by then, and she waited patiently in her breathtaking blue and gray flowered wrap. It looked Hawaiian, and she looked delicious.

"I was thinking"…… I started.

"Uh oh," she teased, her grey eyes dancing, and changing to a brilliant green hue; usually, this is either because she is really happy or really mad.

"I always get nervous when you start 'thinking'!" she jabbed.

"Ha ha!" I laughed a little nervously myself. "Look. I'm serious."

"Ok." And she gave me her full attention. Those beautiful eyes swam in that face that always reminds me of sunshine and strawberries and fire light.

"I was thinking maybe we could take this to the next level."

She looked at me deeply.

I rushed, "I know. I know you decided that you were done with relationships, and marriage, and all of that stuff."

She nodded thoughtfully. We had discussed this several times as friends, when her relationship with Ken imploded.

"Look," I stammered, as she still hadn't said anything. "I mean, I will be your boy toy for as long as you want, if that's what you want. I'm not going anywhere."

I was laid bare before her, my Christian upbringing and pride and my masculinity on the table in front of her. I was all in.

She twinkled as she held back the laughter and said, "Yes, I want to take it to the next level!"

We had the best first date ever, and when we made it to the bed, our clothing did not.

Everything became a team event for the two of us, and I was in heaven. One of our students famously came up to us at an event one time, only having heard our voices on the phone, and said to us each separately, "I bet you guys have GREAT sex!" We both answered her honestly, "Yes, we do!"

The night that Candy and I had sex for the very first time, I had an interesting experience. This guy that had needed to be sure that Karen could not get pregnant - suddenly wanted to be a father. I had never felt that before. With Candy, that night, I felt an overwhelming and deep love for her kids, our kids, Autumn and Nathan and Tasha. I was unsure exactly what to do with it. I suddenly cared who they were dating, how work was going, and if they were ok. And I wanted to have more children with Candy. She had been very sure that she was done having more children after Tasha's birth, and her tubes had been burned and cut to prevent that.

We are working to get the cash to reverse her tubal, because I love having kids; and I have learned to trust that Candy and I are both great parents - and even better as a team.

As much as I have focused on sex in my life, for reasons that go way back in my history, I have learned from Candy that relationship and intimacy is about much more than sex. It's about deep thoughts, and dreams; about listening and supporting, and about celebrating even the smallest of achievements as they happen. I have a book coming out about Candy after this book, as it is impossible to cover her here - all that I have learned and how I have changed with her.

Together, we have found our dream lifestyle in founding The Band Wanted; we travel and sing for a living, and we absolutely love our lives. There is another book about that.

It is an incredibly powerful connection that changes a man like that - and an incredibly powerful woman.

Chapter 16   Autumn Tear

If you have not met Autumn Tear, Candy's eldest daughter, I cannot begin to explain her to you - but I will try. Autumn is fun, deeply compassionate, and she constantly works to unite people. She always has a laugh ready, and she is extremely good at whatever she decides to do. She is a kind and generous hostess, and a marvelous cook. She will make you cry when she shows you how much she loves you. I know, because she loves me. I hope that you get the chance to be in her space, and if you do, when you see how magical she is, give her a hug for me.

I did not always feel this way about her.

When I started dating Candy, Autumn was in Arkansas, with a man that she met online, and married forthwith. Candy did not approve, and the fight was on. This was a pattern for the two of them, as Autumn grew of age and became very dominant and adult. Candy and Autumn fought about every choice that Autumn made.

Enter Joshua into the relationship.

I did absolutely nothing to help at first. In spite of my newly-discovered love for Candy's children, I brought my patterns to the fight. I was terrified of Autumn's free-wheeling dominance, and the chaos that happened in the family anytime that she was involved. I had no respect for her illogical method of choosing, and was even more deeply frightened of the fact that she did not seem to care one bit whether I approved or even liked her.

Of course, many of these traits were the same ones that had attracted me to Candy and her kids in the first place.

Autumn seemed to have a self-destructive bent as well. At one point, she and her self-professed drug-dealer boyfriend were fighting at our kitchen counter - again. The kitchen had been a safe place where all of our kids loved to gather. Candy, with my full support, told Autumn that they could not do battle in our house, and disturb our peace. It was a good boundary. But we were also punishing them, and being extremely right. The result of all of our righteousness was that for two years we did not speak. Autumn missed our wedding ceremony, and we missed the birth of our first grandson, Peyton. It was a horrible price to pay for being right. Autumn, myself, and Candy still cry when we think of the price.

We were choosing the same pattern over and over.

Then one day, for business, Candy and I went to a leadership seminar where I understood the concept of being right vs. being "in relationship" for the first time. I had been so addicted to being right, that I never considered a different choice.

We decided to choose something different that night at the seminar - both of us, independently. And the results are astounding; what I would call a growing relationship with Autumn.

I stopped being "right." I stopped giving Autumn advice. I stopped using my relationship with Autumn's mother over her. I stopped trying to use my approval and acceptance of her as leverage in my relationship with her. I learned that night at the seminar the amazing traits of Autumn's personality type; she was the same personality type as my Grandma Dori, and Candy.

I started loving Autumn unconditionally, and listening; she said that she wanted encouragement, so that is what I gave her. I started finding the positive in her every choice.

I bought her a necklace and earrings, because gifts were important to her. I took a risk and asked her by text if she wanted to do "Father/Daughter Dates," because I read somewhere that it could be an important way to show a girl how she should be treated, and what she could expect from a gentleman. I had been doing this for some months with Candy's youngest, Tasha, and it was a great thing for both of us. Autumn was 24 years old and married, so I felt a bit awkward even asking her. Her texted reply, however, was an instant, "YES."

On those dates, starting from a space of not speaking to each other for two years, Autumn and I developed a true, safe, growing relationship. Some months after we started the dates, I was surprised when she divorced Peyton's father, and began dating other guys again. After months of that, and continuing our dates, I got a text from her, and I could tell that she was crying.

"Why do I keep picking such LOSERS!!!"

I paused in my response. Maybe this was the opportunity I needed to tell her what she had been doing wrong; to give her my valuable advice. Tell her to read her Bible; to only date Christian men; to pray more and ask me before doing anything. But I had been raised that way. And it had not worked very well. So I replied instead with the only thing that I could find that was positive, true, and encouraging.

"But just think how much better this guy was than the last guy!! You are making better decisions!!"

No response. Encouragement, encouragement!

"You are learning, and you are doing it perfectly!"

I distinctly felt the emotions and energy change wherever she was texting me from.

"You are right. I am."

Then, "Thank you, I love you!"

And she was gone. And I still cry when I write about this because it was such a beautiful moment. For both of us.

The next Father/Daughter date was our last, because she spent the whole evening telling me about this Egan fellow. "What is an Egan?" I thought. And there was a small pang of jealousy because I knew. She loved him like she had never loved anyone. I went home and told her mother that this was the guy. I hadn't met him, but I could tell by the way that she talked about him.

Egan

Egan is a red-bearded, extremely creative, and wildly funny man. His GIF wars are epic, his timing impeccable, and he is the best father I could imagine for their kids. He loves Autumn with all of his heart, and has done anything necessary to improve their lives. He and his buddy have started their own business, and he provides many of The Band Wanted's promotional products. He is in a tough business, and he is learning. I admire his intelligence and his commitment. His parents, Joy and Anson, have included our whole crazy family in their events, and I love them and am grateful for them in my life. When I was pre-selling this book, they were among the first to order their copy, making it a financial possibility. I know their hearts; even if they were not interested in the book itself, they would purchase it to show support for me. I am so blessed.

Some months after Autumn introduced me to Egan, I was asked to marry them under a trellis in Joy and Anson's beautiful backyard. We all cried, and the whole family came together in a way that would take your breath away.

I still chat with Autumn Tear as often as possible, support with her homework, hold her babies, and offer coaching if she is stuck and if she asks for support. She loves me deeply and I her. I don't focus anymore on being right; I focus on Autumn.

Even tonight, in 2019, while I am writing this book in the hotel lobby in Pahrump, Nevada, using their free WiFi, 28-year-old Autumn has been reading and proofing my manuscript in the Cloud, and sending me encouragement. She knows me, and she wants me to stop worrying about getting it "right."

She brought tears to my eyes, because she texted me something that I started saying to her over and over about a year ago, when I realized that many of her struggles came from trying so hard to get things right.

She sent me simply,

"Joshua, YOU are doing it perfectly."

Yes, Autumn Tear, obviously I am.

Chapter 17   Nathanuel

Nate. Nathan. Nathanuel. In Hebrew, when you add "el" to a name, it is the suffix of God's name, and it fits Nathan, our middle child, perfectly. I love being around him. Nathan did not need to be so good to this lanky boyfriend of his mom's, but he always has been, because that is who he is. Deeply kind, always the champion of the outcast and the misfit, Nathan is what I would hope a son would be and more than that. I had a special relationship with my Grandpa Bob; we did not gush over each other, or talk a lot, really. We could be very blunt with each other, and neither one of us felt a desire to have drama. We had a deep respect for each other, and we were close in a way that I cannot to this day describe. It is exactly like that with Nathan.

Today, in 2019, Nathan is 26 years old. He was 21 in 2014 when Candy and I started CJ Electric, our own electrical service company. Nate was my first employee, and the best worker I ever had. No fanfare. No demands. Just always there for me.

In between rentals and before meeting his beautiful Sherranne, Nate asked to move back in with us. He respectfully sat both of us down and asked us what would be the deal if he decided to do that. He didn't just assume that he should move back for free; he did not approach his mother on the side, even though I had only been in the picture very recently, and he did not demand that he get special treatment.

It was one of the most honoring things that anyone has done for me, and he set the tone for our family.

Candy and I told him that we would chat about it and give him an answer in a day or less.

We asked him to pay $100 every month for rent, because we wanted him to keep in the practice of paying rent. But unbeknownst to him, I told Candy that I did not want to keep his money. So we put it in a savings account, and when he moved out 11 months later, he got a check from us for $1100. He earned my respect, and I his.

When he lived with us, and before we started CJ Electric, I was in tense wage negotiations with the Union contractors, I would come home stressed-out to the max. He would take one look at my shoulders and face, and say, "You need to kill some people."

I would follow him to his room, and he would let me take half of his TV screen (and really hurt his stellar KD ratio) on Call of Duty, or TitanFall, or whatever new video game that he could introduce me to. He is masterful at whatever he tries, and he has been playing video games for a very long time.

Nathan is fiercely competitive, and almost never loses; but if he feels that his winning is hurting someone, he will pull back and suggest something else. It is rare to find such power and accuracy in a kind and gentle wrapper.

Nathan does not like conflict, and I learned my biggest lesson from him when he was living with us. He taught it to me without saying a word.

There was some drama with Tasha, and I was hurt and angry. I raised my voice at Tash, as I reverted back to what I had learned from my mom. It was the last time I would do that. Nathan did not say anything, but I could feel him losing respect for me at my outburst. It stopped me short. I went to our room, chatted with Candy, talked with Tasha calmly, and then approached Nate's room with fear and trepidation.

Had I lost him forever with my hot-headedness? I did not even respect myself for it now that I had cooled down.

I knelt on the carpet near the foot of his bed where he always sat playing video games.

He looked at me, and there was a new wariness that I did not like to see there.

I didn't know what to say.

"I owe you an apology."

He didn't say anything, but he was listening.

"I was angry at Tasha, and I overreacted. I did not need to yell. It will not happen again."

He nodded slightly, and grunted, just a little bit, as if recognizing that I spoke the truth. His eyes flicked over and I saw a deep pain. I felt horrible for putting that there. I had put his respect for me and his protective love for his sister in competition. I may have cried a little bit. I left his room, knowing that if I truly felt bad, I would show him results. I have not yelled like that again. He calmed our house and taught me a lesson by just being him. He never said a word about it, and never has. He has my back like that.

Sherranne

Nathan was living with us when he began dating an Indian princess named Sherranne from Utah. She is hilarious, competitive, and has a college degree. She has added so much to this family and to Nathan's life.

The first time that Nathan brought Sherranne home to eat dinner with us, I was anxious to make a good impression on this girl. I was bustling back and forth from the kitchen, as I served the chicken enchiladas that Candy was making in the kitchen, and I scooped them onto each plate going around the table. In my awkwardness and hurry, I was mortified to realize that I had run out of enchiladas just as I got to our guest, Sherranne, the love of our son.

There were more in the kitchen; but I froze, unable to think of anything to say. Sherranne, who is a tall, beautiful, dark eyed, Ute Indian, looked up at me and dead-panned in her now-signature fashion, "It's because I'm Native, isn't it." I almost turned inside out for a moment, and then I saw the twinkle way back in her eyes, and we all started laughing. "I like you!" I howled.

If Sherranne is asked her heritage, or is mistaken for a Hawaiian or even for an Asian, she will say "I am this Indian" (two fingers spread like feathers at the back of her head) "not this Indian," one finger stabbing her forehead where a kum-kum would be for a native of India. Or if she is outside when we pull up to her house she will look blankly forward, raise one hand and say, "How."

Sherranne has a great sense of humor, and I could just leave it at that, but underneath her intelligence and fun, is her very soft heart, and her loyalty. She has chosen to be a full part of our family, and be there for anyone who needs her. To open her heart and share what is bothering her, or what she is thinking. She is one of the truly beautiful souls in the world, and my life will never be the same now that she loves me and this family.

As Nate and Sherranne's relationship heated up, we found that he was seldom sleeping in his room anymore, and he had even taken his old Xbox360 over to her place, so he could play it there. We loved her, and the effect that she had on his life, so we were very happy the day that he took his new, top-of-the-line XboxOne to Sherranne's little college cabin, along with his huge flat-screen TV. I knew it was permanent at that point. It was sad to see him go, but it was such pure joy to gain a Sherranne. There is only one like her.

Nate and Sherranne recently bought their first house, and he is maintaining it already like a pro. They also just had their first son, Abel, and they are both such good parents. I shake my head at the love that they are showing each other and that baby. I am so grateful for every day with them.

Chapter 18   Natasha

And then there is Natasha. My little princess. It is 2019, and Tasha is 24. She is our youngest, and she was still at home when I started dating Candy. She and I have a lot of history, and have become very close. In the chaos of my life, I wanted to have children, but after everything that I saw and learned I did not trust that I would be a safe parent. In 2011, as Candy and I joined our lives together, I quickly became involved as a co-parent. And Tasha opened her heart and her life to me. She filled a daughter-shaped hole in my heart. She did not have to.

In fact, The Band Wanted is named what it is because of a conversation with Tasha about family being the people whom you "Want" in your life and who, in turn, "Want" you. I wanted all three of the kids. And Tasha was the one that I got to take back-to-school shopping, and pick up from school when she was sick, and she was the one for whom I got to take time off of work because her tonsils were taken out and she needed special foods and time with me. As time went on, I learned that each of the kids filled a unique spot in my heart; and Tasha was the first one to make a big impact.

The first night that I stayed over with Candy, and before we went to the bedroom, I realized that I was now encroaching on Tasha's home, on her personal space. I was planning to sleep with her mother, and at 17, she was not naive enough to miss what was going on. I approached her on the couch where she was watching TV. She looked at me in that inscrutable way that she does, waiting for me to proceed. I got straight to the point.

"I was thinking of spending the night tonight," I said. Her eyes flickered, but she said nothing.

"I know that this is your home too."

Still nothing.

"I just wanted to ask you if that is ok with you, because if it isn't, I can plan something different."

She looked right at me for a minute. I knew she was gauging whether or not I truly was willing to do something different, or if I was just being polite. I was dead serious.

Her eyes flickered back to the TV.

"It's fine," she said, with finality. She was truly ok with it, but I could feel that it was a good thing that she liked me, because this was definitely against her better judgement.

During the next few years, she and I would get very close. We needed each other, and in an unusual way, she was my first child. She always will be. She is so strong, and so beautiful. She is fiercely loyal, in fact, she is fierce in every way.

Tasha was the only one of the kids to travel with us on the bus, and she was the only other founding member of The Band Wanted. She and Candy and I were very tight travel buddies for a long time, and I dearly miss her out on the road.

I love recording Tasha's music; she goes to a very deep place within herself and she touches me and everyone who hears her when she sings. I look forward to many more projects together. I am excited about her travel van, and the possibilities that stretch out in front of her and Brayden. She is very powerful when she decides to make something happen.

If Tasha is on your side, you will be fine. She will take care of her people. She is way too hard on herself, but she is learning to forgive herself and truly love who she is. When she decides to show you her silly side, which you will never see if she doesn't trust you, you will laugh until you both almost pee your pants. If things get too serious, she will lift a leg and fart at you and you will both laugh until you cry. There are few people that I can spend large amounts of time with, but all three of those kids are that way. I will love them forever, and I am so grateful to Candy and their dad, Gregg, for bringing them to this world.

In 2014, when Tasha was 19 and Nate was 21, Candy and I were given four tickets to watch the Colorado Rockies farm team play in their park located in Grand Junction. We had VIP tickets to the skybox from one of our suppliers to CJ Electric. We took Nate and Tasha both, as they were living at home at the time.

The skybox is a huge area at the top of the stadium, with expansive views of the action. Windows look out both ways; the ones on the west side view the football field and the windows on the east side look out over the baseball diamond.

For the Rockies game, the baseball field side of the box was quickly filling up with tables and chairs to watch the game while enjoying the complimentary food and beverages. We grabbed a table for the four of us, and Candy and Nate and I put chairs around it. We then headed over to the buffet to fill our plates. Tasha wasn't hungry, so she stayed at the huge glass overlook, taking in the game. While we were gone, people that we did not know showed up, and started pushing tables together for their large group. They seemed to need another table, and the big, burly leader of the group decided to just come take ours.

The three of us returned with our plates of food in time to see our 100-pound 17-year-old warrior, clinging like a determined chihuahua to her end of our table, as the big bully pulled so hard on the table that it was literally lifting up off of the floor. And Tasha was not about to give in. Upon seeing us, the brute mumbled something about us not being there to use the table, and stomped off to glare at us and mend his wounded pride.

He just got owned by a fairy nymph with a heart the size of a lion.

That is Tasha. She has my heart and my respect.

Brayden

Tasha has found her Brayden, and I must say that he is a good man. As my princess, I was truly afraid that no one would ever be good enough for her in my eyes. And we have always said that whoever marries Tasha will need to be very different to keep up with her off-the-wall sense of humor. Brayden is all that and a bag of chips. He is a fabulous guitar player, very much fun to be around, and most importantly, he has been everything that she needed from him; always willing to support her in any direction she chooses, for as long as she chooses it. I am still getting to know Brayden, but the fact that he asked a blessing from Gregg, Candy, and I, separately, to marry Tasha, shows a kindness and an intention to respect. I look forward to learning everything about Brayden, and am excited to play piano for them in their wedding in a few weeks.

When we visited them in Lubbock, Texas for Thanksgiving, I went in to their bathroom to pee. As I was standing there doing my business, I noticed that one of Tasha's favorite pictures of the two of them being goofy was over the toilet. For her, a woman, it would not cross her mind; but for a man, it was very disconcerting to be thus exposed and see her face laughing heartily from the picture while Brayden appeared to be leaning toward me with a look of astonishment on his face. I felt very self-conscious. They had a great laugh when I told them about my experience, and they never considered taking it down, because it is too funny. When you can laugh like that, I believe everything will be okay.

Chapter 19　　　　　　　　　Us

Since that first night in 2011, Candy and our beautiful kids have been my antidote. And I have been theirs. It turns out that a safe friend helps to break the silence. Love truly conquers hate, and learning destroys dysfunction.

Every step of the way, the kids have been deeply involved in our relationship. When you join with a woman who has children already, you marry them as well. We asked permission of each of the kids to marry; the girls helped me pick out the ring, and Nathan handed me the box the night that I proposed - because I had no pockets in which to conceal it. These are just a few of HUNDREDS of things that the kids and now their spouses have done to help our relationship move forward. Kids want to have a loving family. If both parents can commit to it, it will happen. I would be an empty shell of a man without this woman, and our kids, and the entire village that has raised them. I am deeply grateful.

Candy found out early in our dating life that I had a large extended family - I had lied and told everyone in Grand Junction that I had no family, because I did not want embarrassing questions. I was putting all the space that I could between me and my past. Candy insisted that I get on Facebook and find them again. She did not berate me for lying to her. She knew intuitively that my heart missed my family. Even the harsh ones. Even the ones who I thought didn't want to hear from me. She insisted, and I tried to tell her that she had no idea what she was letting herself in for. She knows now.

And, I learned something. What Candy's heart knew. I had an awful lot of family members who were still loving me. Friends who had been praying for me for ten years. Family members that did not (and many still do not) understand why I had truly believed that I would not be welcome anywhere in the family because I had "disobeyed" my parents.

I reconnected with my parents as well as all the cousins and aunts and uncles and siblings when Candy convinced me to get on Facebook, although the relationship with Mom and Dad and some of the siblings has broken down time and again.

For a while, in 2012, it looked like everyone was coming to our wedding. There was so much joy and connection. Mom was planning to help with the wedding, and EVERYONE was going to be in it!! I was so excited.

And then something scared my mom. On the phone, Dad said they needed to cancel their involvement because Candy and I were living together before marriage, and that Mom and Dad could not support that. Something about that excuse did not ring true; they had known that we lived together from the moment that we reached out on FaceBook. Something triggered Mom's fear of any turf but her own, and they decided not to go; or maybe they were trying to gain control of our relationship, using their attendance as leverage.

She told all of the siblings to not go. Even though my brothers and sisters had been overjoyed to reunite, they dutifully fell in line; not one of them came to Colorado for the wedding, canceling dress orders, tuxes, and hotel arrangements. The desire to keep the secrets drove the cult to great lengths.

My sister Sarah was the one notable exception. On a seven-year mission to Uganda, and healing in her own way, far away from Eden Road, Sarah cried many tears over not being at my wedding - and would have been, if it were remotely possible. She managed to send a beautiful letter from her in Africa, read by my cousin Renae at my wedding. The love that those two women shared with Candy and I and our wedding guests left everyone in tears and sustains us still.

All throughout Mom's wedding drama, Candy was a rock. She completely re-invented her wedding, and we thoroughly enjoyed my Grandma Dori, Aunt Tammy, Cousin Renae, Renae's husband JBrian Calva, their two kids Olivia and Josiah, and my Great Aunt Mona. Mona took the last trip of her life to my wedding. She passed away months after getting home to Minnesota from complications of the travel. She just wanted me to know that I was loved.

Renae, JBrian, and their young family had no business spending so much money to get out to Colorado; but they were committed to being there for me, so I would know that I was loved. Grandma Dori and Aunt Tammy risked Mom's wrath by letting me know that they loved me. It still makes me cry. Candy created all of that space. When I chose to accept her love, she attracted the real, true, loving people back into my life. Her family showed up and loved on me, and still do.

I cried when she walked down the aisle towards me. Through my tears, I heard Ryan, her cousin's husband (many of her family members work on the oil rigs) saying not so subtly, "Boy, he IS emotional, isn't he?!"

They are honest, blunt, and would give me the shirt off their backs if I asked. They all just want me to know that I am loved. And that I am not alone.

Circles....

In the seminar room, I did an exercise where I drew a large target pattern, with myself in the center. The rings extending outward represented the levels of access that people have to my life; and I, theirs.

It was so enlightening; I had a hard time digesting the concept at first, but it has helped me to this day. In my world of shunning, of "us" vs "them," there had been two options: you were either with us or against us.

Now I realize that there is no "them." We are undeniably on this same planet, and what benefits one, benefits all; and when one hurts, we all hurt eventually.

I get to choose how close I get to every other person on this planet. I get to set boundaries limiting that access, and the give and take of all of my relationships. But I do not have to shun anyone any longer. And I choose to invest fully in each of those circles as appropriate to their distance from me.

Are you on an inner circle? I will give you almost anything if you ask.

Are you on an outer circle? I may have set boundaries with you because you are not choosing to set them for yourself.

Shunning is about controlling you; boundaries are about controlling me and my space, and protecting us both from negative patterns.

This one concept has changed my life. It started with filling my own cup - no one else can know exactly what I need; they are not mind-readers. Next, I focus on extending my energy outward, with intention.

My priorities, and my innermost circle, start with my wife, Candy, and then our kids, and our grandkids. Then outward to my sister, my brother, friends, coaching clients and fans, and eventually to every person that I meet and those that I will never meet. For those like my mother, or Candy's father, we have set boundaries for our safety and theirs. We still love them, though it is at a distance, to limit negative patterns.

I have been asked by many how God, and pastors or counselors factor into this story. My awakening and healing came through a series of personal development seminars, and a whole host of real people who touched my life and set an example for me throughout my life. People who loved me.

Love - that's it; some of them had titles, like pastor or counselor, but the titles were not important; it was their love for me in a real relationship that impacted me the most. AND, I chose to learn from those people, which was the most important factor to my receiving what I needed. Today, you are all my teachers.

I have discovered that when the student is ready, the teacher will appear. So I am the only one who can create the positive change that I want to see in my life.

And I am now committed to being the teacher that others are ready for.

I believe in God, (some have said miraculously, after things that I saw His "people" do) and I have a personal relationship with Him, but I no longer believe in ANY label that people use to make their faith (or mine) a condition of our relationship.

I love you, and that's it. If I want you to perform for me, and make my love conditional, then we are in business, and our relationship is transactional. While transactional relationships may have a place, they are not the highest form of love.

In 2018, before I started writing this book, and after Grandpa Bob passed away, I committed to getting a reconciliation meeting with my parents. Since I do not control their responses, my commitment was to be able to tell them what I loved about them, and valued about them, without dropping into the old pattern of hurling bombs and defending myself.

Through sheer determination, I worked out a way to meet them at Baker's Square, in Mankato, Minnesota, when our tour brought us within 70 miles of the Farm. Candy was there to keep me grounded and calm, and she said almost nothing for the entire two hour meeting.

The meeting started with Mom hurling attacks and doing her best to push my buttons. She was still good at it. I felt the heat rising in my face, as she told me that when Candy and I had been trying to raise money to have Candy's tubes reversed so we could get pregnant, that our asking for money through a Go-Fund-Me campaign had embarrassed her and the whole family.

I was so mad. I was ready to strike back by reminding her of all of the offerings and donations that we received for The Carpenter Family Singers. Candy put her hand on my leg. I took a deep breath and chose to be calm.

If something makes me angry, then there is some truth there for me. I considered this before answering

"You are right." I said, and meant it.

"We tried the Go-Fund-Me page and it just didn't work. We learned something, and we would not do that again."

"Well," Mom said, "we just don't do that in this family; I mean, if we want something, we work for it."

I chose to breathe again. Thank God for Candy.

"No, you are right. The Pullars really didn't like that I was asking them for money," I allowed. "It was a poor way to do it ...but we learned something!" I finished with a grin, feeling the fight in me go down as I agreed with her.

But I did not apologize. I was intent on not sinking back into the old ruts of "fight or surrender."

After she relaxed a bit, it was Dad's turn.

"Joshua, that was not really a big deal to us." (Eye roll here from Mom; he was still not hearing or supporting her) "But I have to know whether you two are saved or not!"

This was what I had been expecting, so I dodged it for a moment. But Dad was not giving up.

I could see that I had to answer this. Now I knew how it felt to be on the other side of the questions that I had posed to Karen at the beginning and end of our relationship.

"Dad," I said, "I am going to answer that, because I see that you have to have an answer. But I really don't want to, and I will tell you why."

But first I turned to Mom, who had taught me about salvation. "Do you really believe that you can be UN-saved?" I asked, incredulously. "You know that I was saved when I was 8, under the stairs in Littlefork, because I told you! Do you think I just lost it somehow?"

She started twisting her napkin nervously. "Well, that is just not for sure, now, there are a lot of questions about that."

I shook my head in disbelief.

"Dad, this is why I don't want to answer the salvation question. Because this is a whole line of questioning that ends relationships. If I say that I am not saved, then I will have to become saved to be in good relationship with you. If I say that I AM saved, then the next question will be some version of, 'Do you believe that the Bible is the inspired, holy, written Word of God?' and if I say no, you can end your relationship with me, but if I say yes, then there is another question.

That question is usually something about how often do I read that Bible ...and it goes on and on until we get to abortion or gay rights or guns and you find a reason that we cannot be in relationship anymore. So that is why I don't like this line of questioning."

Dad was nodding, as if he was listening, but he could not have been. "So, to answer your question, yes, I am saved, and Candy is saved."

Dad feigned relief. "That is good! I am real glad to hear that! Now, my other concern is, do you believe that the Bible is the inspired, written Word of God Himself?"

I thought that Candy was going to choke on her food. She was trying so hard not to laugh in disbelief.

"And I am concerned that you may not be reading your Bible every day," Dad went on.

I looked at Mom. If she realized that this was going exactly where I predicted it would go, she seemed oblivious. She was nodding her head in joint concern about my Bible reading.

"Well, I can tell you that I do not read it much anymore," I said, knowing that this would be all that they needed to shun me again, but deciding to try one more time.

"I read it cover to cover, many times, and one day realized that the whole message is love. And that love is about real relationships with real people, and that rules and being "right" and standing on Bible verses were not helping me to be a better son, or father, or husband. I would rather love you than be right."

They seemed to have no idea what I was saying. I might just as well have had three heads. I was not their teacher in that moment. But they did seem more relaxed, and I was.

The rest of the evening went better, and we even had a few light laughs and pleasant conversation. I was able to tell Mom how much I loved her fun-loving ways, and to tell Dad how much I value his commitment to his convictions, no matter what the rest of the world thought.

Tim and Becky West, who live in Mankato and who had allowed us to shower at their home before the meeting with Mom and Dad, had arranged to come to Baker's Square afterward, in hopes that Mom and Dad might decide to stay and celebrate old times and old friends. Mom and Dad politely declined, saying that they had to get back to the *House of Lights* to dispense medications for the clients. I felt that they really did not want to stay, and I felt sadness for Tim and Becky. I could see that Mom and Dad no longer were friends to them, not really. Maybe they never really had been. I don't know. Tim and Becky stayed with Candy and I, ordered pie with us, and we did celebrate old times and further friendships, and I walked out flying high.

I was sure that Mom would be coming around to a peaceful relationship with me and Candy. I believed that she would be inviting us to Eden Road to show Candy my childhood home, and to relive the good ol' days.

I was wrong. Mom and Dad continued to find reasons and ways to shun us, and there are so many different times and reasons that I am not going to write them here.

Eventually, I realized that I was expending more energy chasing them than I wanted to. And I stopped. The door is always open, but I am no longer trying to force them into my inner circle of influence. I have an absolutely amazing team that has supported me while writing this book. These same people have supported me through every trial and challenge I have encountered, and continue to be there for me. That is why my reviews are not written by accredited professionals. This book is about relationships, so I asked those who know me best, and relate with me on a daily basis, to write my reviews. Those who are in my innermost circle.

Chapter 20
You're Not One Of Us

When Candy was a little girl, growing up in a home where everybody was "saved," but dad was molesting the girls from age 4 until they left home, she had little example or help in going to church. Though her parents profess faith, her dad was intent on hiding the damage that he was doing to his own daughters, and her mom was helping him to hide it.

Even with this strong negative headwind, Candy has a heart of pure, golden sunshine. As her parents uprooted the kids over and over to avoid anyone getting too close, and as she struggled to adjust to new schools and new "friends" that she would never see again after the next move, she took herself to church. She took her younger sisters to church. If she could get a neighbor to give her a ride, or if they could walk, or if a church lady would pick them up in a van, they got their prettiest dresses on and went to church.

She believes.

In spite of all the evidence that she had to the contrary, she believes in good people, and in the communion of those people. She believes in worship, and joy, and love. And church was one place where she found that.

As a result of her running away from home at the age of 14 (and finally telling authorities what her dad had been doing to her) her dad was jailed, and Candy was finally freed. Her allegations were proven by the evidence in court, and she received counselling to help her and her family move on from this awful chapter of her life. She loved the freedom. She was wildly happy.

But she also had a new boyfriend, and he did not understand or know how to deal with her sexual victimization. He may have been himself a victim of a different kind of abuse. In all of that chaos, Candy and Gregg very predictably got pregnant out of wedlock. That baby was Autumn Tear. And the church that had become Candy's port in the storm, her communion of saints, her place of Sunday joy, shunned her.

They did not want "girls like her" to attend their conservative place of worship.

You're not one of us, it's plain to see....

She was heart-broken. Neither Candy nor Gregg were prepared to be parents, and if she ever needed support from women who knew what she was up against, it was then. But they had decided that she did not fit in, for whatever reason. She did not return to a church, and can still experience anxiety when we attend certain churches to this day.

Many church bodies may have handled this situation better; or differently, and one church's choices should not label all churches. That decision, should we make it, is an opposite and equal type of shunning.

This book is not really about the evil of the Carpenter Family, or a church, or Christians, or sexually curious teenage boys. In fact, it is about the underlying human tendency to label, group together, and finally shun the outsider. Shunning can even occur between two people. With only two people, there is a fine line between setting a legitimate boundary for safety - and shunning - and I can only say that my heart knows the difference, and I believe yours does too. Much of my coaching is designed to help the student who is ready to make that distinction. I have an example from my own life of what shunning looks like between just two people.

Grandpa Bob

My Grandpa Bob and I did a lot of really cool things together and I loved him. We fished a lot. I don't even like to fish; but I loved fishing with him. We got firewood, threw hay, and finished many projects together. I cherished the moments that I had with him as a young man. He was a gruff Navy man, and some of the other grandkids that came along after me were afraid of him. I never was afraid of him. Somehow I just understood him. I knew that his bark was much worse than his bite, and that as long as I handed him the wrench when he said, he and I would get along just fine. He was a hard worker, and a truth-teller. He was focused, shrewd, and kept his mouth shut more times than I could have. He embodied the rock-solid patriarch that every family would be so blessed to have as an anchor. He was also an alcoholic.

The fact that he drank more than some only matters because ***of what I did with it.***

In my late twenties, when I left home and became free, I also had to learn to deal with the consequences of my own actions. I got very angry with the failed choices that I was making. I was so determined to prove myself; to be perfect! But I was in a relationship that I had destroyed very early. I was in a job that I did not love. In my zeal to make great choices for myself, I cut off some people and things that had been a source of support for me.

And Grandpa Bob was one of those people. I sent a nasty letter to him, railing at him for "disappearing into the bottom of a bottle," and not being there for me. Whatever he was learning about using alcohol to cope, I decided that it was not valid.

He did not deserve what I did to our relationship. For ten years, I disappeared; I could not be reached, and I did not reach out once. I shunned him.

I chose to use his failings and coping mechanisms as my excuse to sever all ties with him. To punish him.

But whom was I really punishing? It hurt both of us. What had always been mutual respect and a silent understanding, was just a ball of pain and loneliness.

After I met Candy, and my heart began thawing, we attended a self-development class that challenged everything I thought I knew. I was no longer "right." I no longer needed to fight to be "good." I was enough.

This opened up a whole new world of forgiveness and acceptance. I learned that when I am mean and nasty to others, it is always because inside of me somewhere, I am being mean and nasty to me.

What if there was nothing wrong with Grandpa? What if he, like me, was just being himself, with a lot to learn? Surely he should have learned this lesson about drinking by now!! But what if someone else decided for me how long I "should have" stayed in my failed marriage? What if each of us got to decide how long a lesson should take? Was my ten years of misery in that marriage an unforgivable sin? And how should I be punished for that excessive learning time? What if someone cut off relationship with me because of that "excessive" learning time? What if they decided that I would never learn, so I should be left for dead?

I wrote a second letter to Grandpa Bob, ten years later, at the suggestion of one of my mentors in a self-development class. I did not take back my truth. Grandpa Bob was an alcoholic, and we both knew it. I chose to correct what I had done to hurt myself and my grandpa. I told him that whether he drank or didn't, I had always respected him for just being himself, and I also listed some of the incredible things that I had learned just from being near him.

After sending that second letter, I started calling him every Monday morning around 8 o'clock, on my way to work. Grandma Dori told me that I would never know what that second letter and the calls meant to him. "He will run me *over* with his walker to get to the phone on Monday mornings and he hollers, 'That's Joshua, that's for me!'"

Grandpa kept that second letter right by his chair. He was 86 by then.

On Mondays, that gruff old Navy man and I would chat about the weather, or his garden, or the terrible performance of the Minnesota Vikings. At the end of the call I would say, "I love you, Grandpa," and he would say in his brusque way, "Yeh, yeh, I love you too."

I get tears in my eyes just writing this.

It seemed that Grandma was answering my Monday morning calls more often in 2017, and offering reasons that Grandpa couldn't come to the phone. He didn't want me to know that the side of his neck had ballooned with his third bout with cancer in twenty years and that he was tired of fighting.

He passed away in 2017 and I had two years of Monday morning calls to make it easier to let him go. I didn't need a bedside chat as he lay dying. We both knew we were good. It had always been that way between us. He loved me in a way that needed no explanation and never diminished in any way.

In Conclusion

None of us likes to be shunned. We all just want to be loved. Included. Welcomed. Accepted.

I spent many years believing that I was loved only because I was doing my best to be what someone else thought that I should be. When I stopped being what The Carpenter Family Singers wanted me to be, I was shunned, and I tried harder.

Eventually, I left home, but I found other people to try to impress. Other people whose mold I might be able to fit better. Other groups that might not shun me. Still trying to be loved by being what someone else wanted me to be.

I know why people choose bars and homeless camps; sometimes those places have more people who will love them just the way they are than their churches or their homes do.

Now, I am committed to being me. I am a misfit, as Cullen Purser said in the foreword; and I am committed to loving unconditionally.

And I see that everyone else is a misfit as well. There is no mold. Each of us is as individual as a snowflake.

This guy has a different religion than anyone else does; this one has a different sexual orientation. This baby is not born yet, and this woman has had an abortion. This girl is unassertive, and this one dresses provocatively. This child is aggressive, and this one can't focus for very long. This boyfriend has no spine.

All reasons to shun them. Or possibly reasons to love them. I get to choose which one it will be. I choose to love them.

My wife's molester, her father, I choose to love him.

My mother, who has caused much pain in my life; I choose to love her.

My step daughter's dad who seemed so distant for so long, I love him.

And I choose to continue to be me. That is the grand, delicate, terrible, beautiful balance. I choose to be me. And I choose to let you be you.

We will make mistakes, and we will have differences, but this fact was never meant to divide us. Or that we can no longer love each other. Include each other. Welcome each other. Accept each other.

Do you love fun, like Candy and Autumn Tear?

Or maybe you like getting things done, checking boxes off and tracking your accomplishments like my daughter Tasha and her brother Nathan.

Maybe you long for peace and quiet, a good book, a comfortable chair, and a warm drink like me, Egan, and Sherranne.

Maybe you just get drawn into spreadsheets and data, forgetting yourself in processes and configurations that maximize efficiency like my friend Sherri, or my other friend Steve.

I don't have to understand or agree with you to hope that you feel loved. I don't have to be driven by, or even identify with what drives you.

And I can still cheer you on, give you what I have that you may need, and welcome you into my arms, my space, and my heart.

I will set boundaries for my safety, and that will not mean that I don't love you. If you want to be close to me, you will recognize and respect my boundaries. If you do not, then I will enforce those boundaries, and, if necessary, push those boundaries further back.

As Dave Mason says in the song, "There ain't no good guy, there ain't no bad guy, there's only you and me, and we just disagree,"

No matter who you are, you are on my team. Even if we don't agree. Even if we are completely different, or completely opposite.

You're not like me.

You're definitely not like us.

And you are definitely one of us.

Prologue

As this book has come to a close, Autumn has been asking me when I will write another one; I will start one immediately. I love the writing process, and I have had such great conversations and realizations even while writing this one.

I trust that you will read this book in the spirit that it is offered; mistakes were made, and at this point, the only thing that matters is that I learn something from them. I hold no malice towards any of the people mentioned in this book, nor do I pretend to be the final word on this story; I was one of the players, and I have done my best to interpret what I experienced. At the end of the day, it is just that, my experience. It doesn't make me right just because I had this experience, or just because I remember things a certain way.

If you struggled to find a purpose or direction for this book, I can say whole-heartedly, so did I. It was just as confusing to live it. And if it helps, roughly the first half of the book reflects things that didn't work, and the second half reflects some things that did work, with a heavy dose of my learning throughout.

The learning never stops.

We learn best by experience, so if this book has not moved you, get out there and love somebody; I guarantee that you will learn something.

I recommend starting with you.

If this book has moved you, and you would like more, you can find me on Facebook at It's Your Life Coaching.

www.ingramcontent.com/pod-product-compliance
Lightning Source LLC
Chambersburg PA
CBHW030052100526
44591CB00008B/120